Have you ever though about becoming a foster parent? Beth Miller gives you an idea of what you might be letting yourself in for in this hilarious and often moving account of her own experiences. She calls it 'the most frustrating, heartbreaking, exhilarating and rewarding life-style imaginable. Success is great. But success in fostering is special: it comes from being able to say goodbye forever to a child you have grown to love, and welcome a small stranger, all in the space of a couple of days.'

You will meet, among others, Little Lizzy and her temper tantrums; Karen the fifteen-year-old who turns Beth Miller briefly into a foster gran; Glen, a leather-clad rocker with no legs but a definite mission in life – to kill skinheads; and Jane, a severely retarded seven-year-old when she arrives and now a permanent member of the Miller family.

There are about 30,000 foster parents in Britain: you may live next door to one, you may work with one. This book could give you a new insight into what life is like for them and with luck their numbers will be swelled. But even the casual uncommitted reader will come away amused and enriched by such a heartwarming story.

Beth Miller is the pseudonym of a London vicar's wife in her early thirties, with three children and, more often than not, one or two foster children as well.

Room for One More

SURVIVING AS A FOSTER MUM

Beth Miller

JOHN MURRAY

National Foster Care Association

© Beth Miller 1986

First published 1986
by John Murray (Publishers) Ltd
50 Albemarle Street, London W1X 4BD

Typeset by Inforum Ltd, Portsmouth
Printed and bound in Great Britain
by Richard Clay, The Chaucer Press, Bungay, Suffolk

British Library CIP data
Miller, Beth
    Room for one more: surviving as a foster mum.
    1. Foster parents — Great Britain
    I. Title
    362'.7'33'0924   HV887.G5

ISBN 0-7195-4342-8

Contents

The illustrations are by Michael Bartlett

For the real 'Helen',
with my love

Preface

This is the story of a foster family; *our* family. It is uniquely our story, not an example of what to expect or a treatise on the drawbacks and benefits of being a foster parent. The tears and triumphs are different for everyone. There can be no uniformity in experience, for human beings simply don't work according to rules or patterns. A flavour, a taste of the real thing is all that I can share; *that* I do gladly.

I

And Why Begin?

I tilt my head, clamping my ear to the telephone. Both hands are busy feeding the baby. He in turn is passing it all on to Teddy.

'Look, I'm sixteen now,' the voice at the other end protests indignantly. 'It's *my* business if I want to stay out all night. Besides, Andy might be too drunk to drive me home after the party.'

Andy, I reflect bitterly, is no different drunk than when sober. Just as I am about to point this out, the baby manages to throw his bowl across the room. It lands – face down, of course – on the carpet. Banana on brown.

This is the very moment chosen by the eight-year old to burst through the door as an authentic Indian warrior in full battle cry. The war paint looks impressive – and familiar. Ah, yes. I last saw it on my dressing table, in expensive little pots.

After we had been fostering for a while, you did not have to be a Sherlock Holmes to spot that ours was the home of a foster family. It was not over-large, but it was full. Visitors found their every move watched by wide eyes of various shades and shapes. Sitting

on the sofa, they were almost guaranteed to be the ones who found the half-finished sweet.

There was evidence of future budding artists on the walls and, here and there, an odd piece of wallpaper missing, where an enthusiastic but unknowing hand had decided to help with the decorating. There were crumpled clothes on the bathroom floor and, most important of all, a steady beat of noise.

Now, all this could apply to any family where there are several children. What gave us away as being a foster family was not so much who *was* visible, as who wasn't. In a family of schoolchildren, for instance, why was there a pram under the stairs? Sometimes the place was awash with babies, not a tube of acne cream in sight. So, who hid the packet of cigarettes behind the cistern?

As hosts, my husband Chris and I were one of the most relaxed couples you could wish to meet, and made our visitors feel instantly at home. It would be comforting to be able to say this was because we are such warm, charming people. This is not quite the case.

There comes a point, a bit like the aerobic pain barrier, where tiredness transcends the bounds of social nicety. It is at this point impossible to care whether your guests are impressed. You only want to know if they can change a nappy. And Atilla the Hun would have been welcome in our house sometimes, to create a diversion for an adventurous toddler while Mum indulged in the luxury of going to the loo all by herself.

Why did *we* begin it? We have been asked that question so many times. Sometimes it arises out of pure interest, sometimes as a test of our mental capacities. After all, if we cannot answer, 'Well, we fell into it by accident, really'; if we actually *chose* to lumber ourselves with other people's children, we shall prove ourselves an odd couple.

Indeed, foster parents are still rare enough to have a definite novelty value at parties.

'Have you met Beth and Chris? They're foster parents. Here, get them to tell you about the time when . . .'

We will usually oblige. But, to people not closely involved with our family, we never use real names, and we never disclose meaty details of why children have come to us.

'To protect the innocent,' says Chris, always with a wry smile. Some of our children have been far more knowing than us.

Before we became foster parents we were as innocent babes, although we did not know it. Reared in the suburbs of London less than half a mile away from each other, we had pursued our joint path through the same schools and then on to an early marriage and the same University town. Chris took up his first professional post, as Vicar in charge of a small inner-London congregation, just before our daughter was born. And I put my teaching degree on ice for a while, and looked forward to being the hub of a small, happy family. I would bake, and sew, and grow plump and contented while my babies blossomed around me. In those days, we talked in plurals. It was a few weeks after Helen's birth that we began to see the overwhelming advantages of being a one-child family.

So why *did* we begin it? It is a question I ask myself, too, and have never yet found a satisfactory answer for. We had always talked about it, even before we were married. It was a simple extension of an impulse to share, to give back to the world a little of the joy we had found there. Sounds dead noble, doesn't it? But noble feelings tend to disappear when an insecure three-year-old invades your bed for the umpteenth night running with, 'I gotta sleep wiv you – there's *fings* in my bed *again*.' Fostering may well uplift the soul. It does very little for your love-life.

Perhaps, then, it is better to just plunge in with a taste of life in a foster family. In telling the stories of our children perhaps our own story, that of an ordinary couple living a sometimes extra-ordinary life, will show itself – at least to me.

The triumphs and tears of caring for 'second-hand children' are very finely balanced. We fostered many children in a relatively short space of time. Not all of them are remembered with the same fondness. Along the way, we acquired a daughter, who came to stay for a couple of months, 'until a permanent home can be found'. She never left, and now shares not only our home but our name. We almost acquired a son, too, and still feel the echo of an ache when we recall the 'almost' that never quite made it to an actual.

But I digress. I will save their stories for later. In those first, tentative days we had only Helen, our first-born and our treasure beyond price. A baby of ten months when we took that first step towards being foster parents, by the time she was six Helen was an old hand at the business. She knew all the technical terms and pretended to have read all the books. For Helen, expanding your family became a very simple matter. 'Oh you can make your own baby of course, but that takes time, and it's a bit chancy, particularly if you fancy a BIG brother or sister, who can take you to the park and feed you sweeties. No, far better to place your order with your Social Worker.'

Helen is as good – and bad – as the next child, but there is an extra dimension to her experience and therefore her personality. She has seen far too much to take her comfortable home and loving parents for granted. Helen is irrepressibly buoyant. Her full charge into life leaves her parents exhausted.

Like us, Helen has loved some of her foster brothers and sisters more than others, but she has learned from them all. And always, when she talks of her own hopes for marriage and a family, there is room for a foster child or two. For this we breathe a sigh of thanks. Despite our fears, growing up in a weirdo family has done her no harm and nurtured no bitterness.

On that first day, when I picked up an electoral registration card from the doormat and saw the post-mark advertisement, 'Foster a Child' with a phone number, I picked up the telephone on impulse. We had always talked about doing it 'one day'. There could be no harm in asking for more information.

Within a week, Chris and I were sitting on the edge of our living room sofa, gripping a steaming mug of coffee each. Across the room sat a Social Worker, also gripping a coffee, also sitting on the edge of his seat. His name was Neil.

This little scenario, with slight variations in the cast-list, was to become a routine part of life for us over the years. It would always mark the ritual beginning of discussion, review, or the placement of a new child. This first meeting was embarking us on a voyage that would stamp and change us for ever.

We knew nothing of this as we sipped our coffee and talked. We only wondered why Neil, who had explained that his job was to get to know us intimately, looked even more nervous than Chris and I.

2

The Real Thing

Over the next few weeks we were to meet Neil several times, and grew to like and respect him very much. He was newly qualified, a bit nervous, and anxious to 'do things properly'. But his perception and gentle wit made him very easy to talk to. And there was a lot of talking to do, as he questioned us about our childhoods, our hopes and ambitions. Neil watched us talking to Helen, and each other – it was his job to somehow assess us as a family, how stable we were. Some of the questions he asked us took us by surprise.

Chris, an ordained clergyman, was asked whether he would expect our foster children to go to church. He decided it was not the sort of thing he would want to force upon anyone old enough to express an opinion. I was asked if the experience of my parents' divorce, when I was a small child, would make me better or less able to cope with children from a similar situation. I replied, quite honestly, 'I've never thought about it – I don't know.'

Far from being the third degree we feared, these sessions came to be quite an amusing diversion for Chris and I. Never before had we actually sat down and looked at what made us 'tick' as a family. We began to surprise each other with some of the things we said; how different we were.

Chris, outwardly quiet and reserved, is commonly supposed to be the shy one.

'In fact,' he explained to Neil with relish, 'I just don't speak unless I have something to say – unlike Beth. *She's* the one who doesn't like being in a crowd, so she prattles on to cover up. No-one is given the chance to catch up with her. Beth couldn't sit still with her mouth shut to save her life.'

'Oh Chris!' I protested as I jumped up to pour some more coffee. 'That's not . . .'

'You see?' crowed my loving husband.

Another difference between us is in how we control our anger. My quick temper and explosive outbursts are in marked contrast to Chris's icy calmness.

'But at least my moods are short-lived,' I said. 'It may take ages, but when Chris finally decides to blow, everybody had better stand well back. No use going back to examine the embers, either. He sulks for *ages*.'

'All right, quits,' said Chris.

'Quits,' I agreed.

What it all boiled down to was that Chris and I are like chalk and cheese when it comes to temperament.

'That's no bad thing, you know,' Neil pointed out. 'After all, you complement each other. The important thing is whether your attitudes, your ideas about where you're going and what you want, are the same. Don't you think so?'

We had to agree it made sense.

We covered everything in those talks with Neil. Any moment I was expecting to be asked what brand of toothpaste we preferred, or our views on Australian cricket. Finally, though, it was over, and we settled back to wait. The Fostering Panel would consider our application, together with Neil's reports and references from close friends who knew us as a family. We had chosen Helen's godparents, and the Vicar who supervised Chris through the latter part of his training.

The vetting was a long haul, especially in our case. We moved house, Chris changed jobs, and then we all in turn caught 'flu. Added to this were all the problems of finding times when all three of us were free. Instead of a couple of months, it was just about a year before Neil was ready to submit our application. On reflection, we felt this was no bad thing in any case. It was better to wait until Helen was a little older.

Waiting to hear plunged us back to those long hot summers before examination results. When The Letter finally arrived, we were as excited as kids at a birthday party. We were now approved foster parents, recommended age group 5 – 9 years. We were also members of the National Foster Care Association, and their latest magazine was enclosed.

'I wonder when we'll get our first child,' I mused.

'Soon, if they're as desperate as they say,' said Chris. 'We'll find twins and a cat on the doorstep tonight, I shouldn't wonder.'

'They must be *really* desperate,' I said sarcastically after several weeks. 'Look how they're beating a path to our door.'

Chris shook his head. 'I don't understand, either. Maybe we should call Neil and find out if our name has actually been added to the register of foster parents. They may have missed it somehow.'

In fact, we were discovering right at the beginning one of the basic frustrations of being a foster parent. You can be weeks – even months, sometimes – without a child. Then suddenly you get whammed from all directions. Neil told us there had been several enquiries – requests were supposed to go to him, not to us directly at first – but he was waiting for a straighforward case to start us off.

'We're just keen to get going,' I said. 'Anyone will do, honestly.'

'You'll learn,' muttered Neil darkly.

Meanwhile, there was the inevitable Medical to get through. When we got the forms through the post we could hardly believe it. It was a standard medical form, for use by all prospective foster and adoptive parents. We were to take it to our local G.P. Chris and I perused it in awe. Helen, sitting in her high chair, tucked into her porridge with both hands. There was no point in making life difficult with spoons when Mum and Dad were not looking.

'Here, Chris,' I looked up from my soggy toast. 'What on earth does "Is natural parentage contra-indicated" mean?'

'It means, are we able to have children of our own,' he said. 'Physically, that is,' he added, looking pointedly at Helen. 'Thankfully, they're not asking about whether we're mentally ready for another one like this little muck-heap here.'

Helen, realising she was once more the centre of attention, gave a huge grin. A dollop of porridge fell from her cheek.

'I suppose that bit's for adoptive parents really,' I said. 'Makes a difference to your position on the waiting list, or something.'

'Never mind all that,' said Chris. 'How's your MCU? Or your CNS?'

'My what?'

Chris grinned at me over his form. 'It's all here, you know. There's even a space for the wetness of your nose.'

'Where?' For a moment I almost believed him. 'Oh Chris, stop it. What page are you on?'

'Two.'

'Well, go half way down page three.'

'Mmmmm . . .? Oh, I see. Well, I can tell you just how I feel about strangers taking liberties with *my* posterior – yuk!'

'So, do we really want to do this, Christopher?'

Chris put down his form and slowly drained his cup. 'Well,' he said finally. 'At least we'll know we're healthy. If we are, I mean. Top to toe, we'll glow with health and vitality.'

'If we survive it,' I added. A blob of marmalade slid off my forgotten toast and landed splat on the plate. I did not feel hungry any more. 'Ah well. Onward and upward, Carruthers. Face it like a man, etc. etc.'

'That's the spirit,' said Chris.

We attended the Medical together, trying to appear very nonchalant and casual about the whole thing.

Our doctor was a very short, rotund Scots woman who smoked like a chimney, even in the Consulting Room. We were a healthy family and rarely needed to consult her. This was fortunate, for her approach to medicine was a little more *laisser faire* than I felt comfortable with. My last visit had been with a throat infection.

'God, what a mess!' had been Dr Kincaid's comment on examination. 'Nothing I can give you, though. Viral, you see. Painful?'

I nodded dumbly.

'Gargle wi' a good drop o' Scotch. Then swallow it – ye'll sleep, if nothing else.'

As we trooped into the Consulting Room this time, and handed over the forms, Dr Kincaid pushed aside her ashtray and gave vent to a hacking cough. Then she disappeared behind the forms.

'Good God!' came an exclamation.

I shifted nervously in my seat. Chris suppressed an uneasy laugh. The forms were lowered. Dr Kincaid peered at us over the rim of her bi-focals.

'Good God,' she said again. 'It's the works, eh?'

'Yes,' I grinned sheepishly.

'A real going-over they want, is it?'

'Yes.' I swallowed.

'I've never seen anything like it. Have you?'

We answered in miserable unison. 'No.'

Dr Kincaid thumped the forms down and rummaged for her stethoscope.

'Never you fear, lass. You just tell me – are you healthy, d'you think? Both of you?'

Startled, we nodded.

'Aye, I think so too. So I'll tell you what. We're goin' to do the essentials – heart, lungs, that sort of thing. And then we'll just *tick* the rest o' the ridiculous thing. It's a load of rubbish, and I'll tell them so. *I'm* not examining anybody's anus to see if they can be foster parents!'

And so it was over. The forms were sent off, together with Dr Kincaid's no doubt ribald comments on the relevance of some of the questions. She was presumably not the first – much later, I heard there was a move to 'rationalise' the whole business of Medicals. We half-expected a letter, telling us the whole thing would have to be done again. No such letter came; instead, we had a telephone call from Neil.

'We've a possible placement for you – brother and sister, aged six and eight. Mother in hospital. Interested?'

'Oh yes,' I breathed. We were off, at last.

Nadia and Glenroy lived with their mother on the other side of the borough. She had come to Britain from Guyana as a young bride, only to be deserted by her husband when the children were tiny. There were no friends or family to entrust her children to, so when an operation became necessary Nadia and Glenroy had to come into care. This had happened before, and the children were well prepared for a short stay away from home. They came to us quite eagerly, anticipating a lovely holiday. It was the sort of trouble-free placement foster parents dream of, but rarely see.

We had a simply glorious fortnight. It was towards the end of the summer. The weather was balmy. We went to the zoo, and the seaside. Nadia and Glenroy were our very first foster children and they hold a special place in our memory. They were bright, exuberant, curious creatures.

Never will I forget Nadia's wide-eyed amazement when we drove from our home in the centre of London to visit family in Buckinghamshire. As we reached the Green Belt, Nadia tapped me urgently on the shoulder.

'Is Mr Callaghan still Prime Minister *here*?' she asked. She was eight years old, and had never left the grimy, tree-less streets around her home. To her, Suburbia was another country altogether.

Glenroy had a roguish charm all his own.

'I *like* it here. The last foster mother had horrid lumps in the mashed potato . . . she *made* us eat it,' he confided as he tucked into his dinner the second evening.

The flame of pride in my eye was quickly quenched with his next remark. 'Mind you,' he said, prodding my 'Italian Casserole' suspiciously with his fork. 'she never gave us these black lumpy things. What *are* they, anyway?'

Helen thoroughly enjoyed the extra attention. She was pronounced, 'sweet' and 'cute', and therefore well worthy of a game of chase or peek-a-boo. They would have played non-stop if Chris and I had had the stamina to withstand the shrieks of laughter.

When Nadia and Glenroy finally left us we were exhausted but satisfied. Apart from the odd squabble and argument about bedtimes, there had been virtually no problems at all. We felt fuller, rounder somehow, with the sense of achievement of a job successfully completed.

'They were great, weren't they?' said Chris as we settled into each other's arms the night after returning Nadia and Glenroy to their mother.

'Mmmm. I don't know what we were so anxious about, Chris. I mean, we coped rather well, didn't we? I think we'll enjoy this fostering lark.'

'Yep, it's our natural niche in life, I reckon.'

'Nothing to it.'

Like cossetted infants, we snuggled down into self-congratulatory slumber, to dream of further wonderful experiences with further charming children.

We had a lot to learn.

3
Little Lizzy

After Nadia and Glenroy left, we faced another fairly lengthy break. A couple of children came to stay for a night or two, 'in transit' to somewhere else. Our contact was so brief it is hard to recall their faces now. We were working up to our first long-term placement, and sure enough along it came. Alison, or Lizzy as she was known, would be with us for some months. It seemed a little bit daunting, and we were waiting apprehensively in the living room long before the expected time of arrival.

When the doorbell rang, I sprang to my feet. 'That must be them.'

Our smiles hid the uneasiness that would always beset us as we greeted a new foster child. That moment before the first impressions were formed, as the front door opened, was like waiting in the wings for your cue, or the single shivering moment at the side of a cold pool, before the first dive.

Janet Graves, a Social Worker we had met once or twice before, held a tiny, exquisite little girl with polished black skin and dark, glowing eyes.

'Hallo. I've brought Lizzy to stay with you.'

'Lovely,' I smiled. 'Come on in.'

I bent slowly to welcome Lizzy, and she clung nervously to Janet, thumb planted firmly in mouth.

As we all sat down, Helen came bounding down the stairs. Helen was then, as she is now, a creature of superlatives. Helen never walks, but bounds; she is never content or annoyed, but outraged or overjoyed. Difficult perhaps, especially at the end of a hard day, but never boring. Excited at the prospect of a new playmate, she shot into the room like a bullet, with a 3000 megawatt smile and shout of welcome that could split the atom.

Lizzie looked justifiably horrified as Helen bore down upon her, flung herself onto the sofa and asked, 'How old are you?'

Lizzy just stared.

'She's three and a half,' Janet answered for her.

'I'm four and a bit,' Helen was superior. 'Do you want to see my toys?'

She stretched out a dimpled hand. To my surprise, Lizzy allowed herself to be pulled away from Janet, who smiled at her reassuringly and then relaxed against the cushions as Helen led Lizzy up to her bedroom.

'Thank God for your Helen,' laughed Janet. 'She cuts the introduction time by half! Now, I'm sorry I couldn't tell you much on the phone, but it was a bit of a surprise to us all.

'We had a call from the court this morning. Lizzy's mother had just been sentenced to one year's imprisonment. *Then* they found out, much later, there was a child waiting to be picked up from nursery school. Apparently, she told no-one about the court appearance, or made any arrangements about Lizzy.'

'I suppose she expected to go free?' queried Chris.

'I expect so,' Janet nodded. 'Wishful thinking, unfortunately. It's not her first offence. Anyway, the teacher at school took Lizzy home with her, and I met her for the first time when I went to pick her up an hour ago. It's a shambles, really – I don't know what can be going on in the little mite's head. I've explained as much as I can: she's taken it all very calmly so far, I must say.'

'What about her mother?' I asked.

'Carol is in Holloway at the moment – she'll be sent to an open prison up north next week. We expect her to be away at least eight or nine months. We will arrange for Lizzy to visit, of course, but it will be difficult to do much at that distance.'

'Did you manage to find out about Lizzy's routine and so on?' asked Chris.

Janet nodded briskly. 'Not much, but I spoke to the teacher. There is a father, but he rarely appears – doesn't live with them. She likes sausages and painting. Usually she's very sweet.'

'Usually?' I pounced on the slight stress. 'Isn't that social work jargon for, "And now the bad news"?'

Janet smiled. 'As ever. She can be a handful, and has wailing tantrums; she kicks and bites and so on. Her teacher seems to think that experience of a stable family life will help that problem –

you never know your luck.'

'On the contrary,' said Chris gloomily, 'I know our luck only too well. With *our* luck, she'll teach Helen these endearing little ways and we'll have them both at it.'

At that moment the two girls could be heard coming down the stairs, laughing together. The came in hand-in-hand, having clearly struck up an instant friendship; Chris and I exchanged relieved smiles.

We all went to the gate to see Janet off. Lizzy had been very composed up to now, but as soon as Janet's car disappeared she howled like an abandoned wolf cub. Chris carried her into the house, attempting to soothe her without success. Lizzy threw herself on the floor and pounded our rug with all her might and fury. I sat on the floor beside her – she would not be touched – and allowed the storm to run its course. Chris cuddled Helen, who was wide-eyed and serious. As the sobs began to die down, I gently tapped Lizzy on the shoulder.

'Hey, Lizzy. Mop up your face – you'll be washing the carpet soon. And I need your help. We have to go to the butcher's and choose something for dinner.'

'Sausages?' queried Chris.

'Sausages, chips and beans?' beamed Helen.

'Hmm. We'll see.' I winked at Chris as Lizzy's sobs stopped in mid-flow and she dabbed inexpertly at her nose with my handkerchief.

'Are we going now?' It was the first time she had spoken. While the girls went to get their coats, Chris and I hugged each other.

'First hurdle over,' he murmured.

Over the next few days, Lizzy seemed to settle remarkably well. She and Helen quickly became inseparable. They took to sharing an armchair to watch TV. At night they talked and sang together until their eyelids just became too heavy.

Lizzy's bed was wet every morning, but this was the only sign that she was less than happy. It amazed me that Lizzy could apparently lie between wet sheets quite happily, even after she woke up in the mornings. However, with true text-book parenting I did not comment, but merely provided her with clean sheets and told her to put the soiled ones in the washing basket.

'Thank God for the washing machine at least,' I remember thinking, the day before it broke down.

The girls begged to be dressed the same, and were delighted with the little dresses I made for them, alike in every detail. Both exhibitionists by nature, Lizzy and Helen basked in the exclamations and amused glances of passers-by in the streets. They even tried to pass themselves off as twins, with a typical child's ignorance of colour and the laws of genetics. Once, on a long train journey, they gave an impromptu concert and the lavish song and dance routine went on with no concern at all for my embarrassment. Their performance gave a whole new meaning to the idea of black-and-white minstrels.

Sometimes, Lizzy would wake at night and come into our bedroom for a little cuddle. I would awake with a start in response to her hand on my shoulder, and see nothing in the pitch darkness except two white circles with dark centres, gleaming brightly above flashing white teeth a couple of feet from my face. It never failed to un-nerve me.

I steeled myself for trouble in those early days but it didn't come. The biggest problem, in fact, was not Lizzy's behaviour but her hair. It seemed the same texture, almost exactly, as a fleece. I had been given the local authority leaflet on 'Caring for Black Children', and I studied it avidly. It told me nothing I had not absorbed from my own black and Asian friends – none of whom, as luck would have it, lived near enough to help me out. I was told by the West Indian nursery assistant at Lizzy's school to keep her hair oiled, and dutifully bought some foul-smelling concoction at the local chemist.

Then Beverley, a West Indian teacher I had studied with, came for a visit. Proudly I showed her the pot I had bought. With a look that spoke volumes, she pointed to the bin.

'What's wrong with it?' I asked. 'The chemist said it's the stuff.'

'There's nothing *wrong* with it,' she said. 'It's just inappropriate. It would be like you using your Grandad's Brylcream to set *your* hair.'

'It cost nearly two pounds!' I protested.

Beverley's finger never wavered. In the bin it went, and I followed her to a shop that sold many more sweet-smelling products.

The oil, once massaged into Lizzy's scalp, did make her hair easier to handle. The comb finally worked, and Lizzy's hair seemed less like a fleece and more like liquid plasticine. Wherever you put it, it stayed, though its natural inclination was to stand straight up in the air.

At first, Lizzy had her hair done at school, by the nursery assistant. Then half-term approached. Beverley came again, and showed me a few basic styles to try at home.

'There you go,' she said. 'It's down to you, next time. You have to try it sometime, Bethy.' The prospect clearly amused her.

The next morning I set to work with enthusiasm, Lizzy patiently munching on a piece of toast. Two-and-a-half hours and many bribes and tears later, I finished. Though the final creation bore no relation to what I had been shown, I was quite proud of the result. Lizzy clearly thought I was an incompetent idiot. She looked in the mirror at my masterpiece and said enigmatically: 'I've never had it like *that* before . . .'

The saving grace of a black hair style is that, once done, it stays for at least a couple of weeks. Indeed many black women who have the most complicated styles keep the plaits in much longer than that, washing their hair with the style somehow intact. I never got

the hang of that. Lizzy's hair was done every ten days or so. It was a marathon task and a family effort, with Chris reading stories and Helen fetching and carrying toys to try and make the time go a little more quickly. By the time Lizzy left us I had refined my technique to the point where it took only forty-five minutes – I watched her mother do it in ten, and it looked a lot better too.

Meanwhile, I became a clandestine head watcher, always on the lookout for new ways to plait Lizzy's hair. On tubes and buses I sat near black women whenever possible, peeping out from behind my newspaper and staring whenever I thought I could get away with it. One style, 'cane row', was very much in vogue at the time. I was never able to master it, even after many hours of contriving to queue behind it in supermarkets.

As summer approached I took to wandering down the High Street with the girls every Saturday, leisurely strolling round Woolworths while they scrutinised the toys and daydreamed about Christmas and birthdays, all impossibly far away, and window shopping. Lizzy and Helen liked going shopping very much, particularly on a Saturday when the rules about sweets were relaxed and they were allowed to stuff themselves before lunch. On one such occasion I was looking in the window of the local stationers, trying to decide whether my need of a felt-tipped pen was great enough to make me join the lengthy queue.

A voice shouted something behind me.

'Go back where you came from, the lot of you. Damn nigger brat!' A drunk, surely. I whirled round. No, the woman seemed sober enough. Nor did she have the wild stare of a psychotic. She knew what she was saying, all right. And she was addressing herself to three-year-old Lizzy. The woman pointed a gnarled finger at her, ignoring her terror.

'You got no right to be 'ere, takin' bread out of white children's mouths.'

I gripped both the girls tightly by the hand, aware of the anguish on Helen's face, and Lizzy's rigid little body. My voice was feeble.

'Leave her alone,' I said. The poison came my way.

'And you're no better than you oughta be, taking in a nigger's child. They should all be sent back where they came from.'

I was beginning to recover a little from the shock. 'Fine,' I replied acidly. 'I'll put her on the next bus to Tottenham.'

The sarcasm was completely lost and the woman barely paused in her abuse.

Quite a few people had gathered by now – big strong arms suddenly slipped around Lizzy and lifted her up.

'Don't you take no notice, lovey,' a man was saying. 'She's mad, the old coot.' And Polo mints, one of Lizzy's favourites, were produced as if by magic.

'Shut your foul mouth,' another woman was shouting at our attacker. 'You poisonous old cow!'

As more onlookers turned on the woman, she literally backed away from us and stamped off down the street, muttering indignantly. She was followed by hostile stares from other shoppers.

Helen had remained absolutely silent, though tears ran down her cheeks. She shook her head when someone offered her a chocolate bar. Lizzy, who had not really understood what the woman was saying, only the anger behind the words, was solemnly chewing sweets in the arms of a strange man.

'Don't you take no notice, my dear,' someone was repeating through the cotton wool that filled my head. 'She's got to be a nutter.'

But I had seen her face and looked into her eyes. I knew she was as sane as I. We were complete strangers to her, my two little girls and I. Yet she hated us all. Although I was a mature woman, six years married, the cruel truth about racism hit me, as it must hit children, for the first time. I did not understand.

Our shopping expedition spoilt, we joined hands and went home. It was not until I recounted our ordeal to Chris, shaking with futile rage, that I realised there was beauty even in this ugliest of human encounters. One person had screamed abuse; a dozen more had stayed to defend and support us. It was a cheering thought, and my faith in humanity began to heal.

It was, however, at about this time that things began to go wrong with Lizzy. The first tantrum hit us out of the blue, without warning. After a riotous game of hide and seek one evening, both girls ate hungrily. Lizzy drained her glass of milk and held it up.

'More drink?'

Automatically I waited pointedly for the 'please' and did not respond. When Lizzy reached across the table for the milk jug, Chris playfully caught her hand. 'You've forgotten something.'

Lizzy looked at him angrily.

'Please . . .' he prompted gently: the sort of farcical domestic scene which every mother who has had to teach her child manners will recall only too well. But Lizzy's dark eyes, as she raised her head to look Chris full in the face, held an unquestionable challenge. Silently, Helen and I carried on with our meal, though my stomach tightened. The ear-piercing scream which followed made me drop my fork in astonishment.

Lizzy had knocked her chair over and was on the floor. There she remained, wailing and screaming by turns and drumming her feet on the polished floor. Helen looked on, open-mouthed, as Chris shouted:

'Lizzy! Stop this at once!'

The wailing, if anything, increased. Chris turned to me. 'Open the door.' He picked up the kicking bundle and took her into the hall.

'You can come back in when you're quiet, madam, and not before.' He set her on her feet. '*We* are going to finish our dinner.'

Chris shut the door and returned to the table. We all picked up our forks and ate, not tasting the food. Lizzy's protests seemed to be reaching a crescendo, then they gradually died down.

'What now, Chris?'

'Carry on as normal.'

'Ignore it?' I could hardly believe my ears.

'What else can we do? Anything else would give her a victory, wouldn't it? After all, it's attention she's after.'

'Straight out of Spock, no doubt,' I said sarcastically.

Chris pushed his plate away and his face flushed with anger.

'Look, Beth, I'm not going to create a fight between us. So, my idea is no good – what do *you* suggest?'

I knew he was right. I was striking at him to relieve the anger I felt at my own helplessness.

'I'm sorry,' I said. 'Let's hope this is the finish of it.'

But Lizzy was only just beginning, and that evening marked the start of a series of wild and unpredictable bouts of temper. The tantrums were sudden and unavoidable. As the days wore on they seemed to get worse: Lizzy would kick and try to bite anyone who came near her.

She reserved her best shows for the days when we had visitors, who provided her with a new audience, shocked and horribly embarrassed. Chris and I became very good at brittle jokes and assumed indifference to the muffled thuds and wails which could be heard after Lizzy's inevitable removal from the sitting room, while our guests carefully pretended they couldn't hear a thing. Afterwards, when all was quiet, I would take Lizzy in my arms and try to cuddle her. Invariably she would turn away and curl up on the floor, preferring even that cold, hard surface to me. If Chris were home she would go to him, climbing onto his lap and snuggling down with a tiny smile of triumph as she looked at me. Gradually I realised what lay at the roots of these tempestuous rages – jealousy. Lizzy could not bear to be anything but the centre of attention. The tantrums, which had seemed so unpredictable, had a pattern after all. Whenever our attention was diverted to someone else, Lizzy would go into action. She was especially jealous of contact between Chris and myself, and our slowness to recognise this particular facet was what had made her behaviour so unpredictable. A kiss on the cheek, holding hands on a walk, a shared joke: all would be cues for tantrums, screaming, kicking and biting anything or anyone in her path. I began to wake in the mornings with my teeth clenched, and the thought of the approaching school holidays filled me with dread. Lizzy would be at home all day then.

Chris and I argued constantly, it seemed, over little things. We were unconsciously staying away from each other so as to avoid 'Setting Lizzy Off', though it took a while to realise that. At the time, we were aware only of a change in our relationship and our irritation with each other. We looked forward to the holiday we had booked on a Somerset farm – surely, with so much to see and do, Lizzy would be distracted.

Not a bit of it. The tantrums became worse still, a combination of a change in routine which left Lizzy insecure, and the fact that Chris and I were together much more. I saw that Lizzy was quite pepared to share us both with her foster sister; there was no sign of jealousy when Helen was cuddled or attended to – but Lizzy was not prepared to share Chris with me. I realised, too, with a sinking feeling of guilt and knotted misery, that actually I did not *like* Lizzy, even when she was at her best. She could be so sweet and charming – a real little doll, people would say – but there was no affinity between us. I tried hard not to show it, but perhaps she knew that, deep down, I was counting the days.

This guilt was difficult to deal with. I had expected, when we started, to love each and every child equally, as if my own maternal outpourings would flow from a brimming jug onto the eager little hearts who waited to lap them up, regardless of personality differences. Today, I realise how unrealistic this was; at the time it seemed not only reasonable but essential. And I very much disliked this cute angelic looking child. Meanwhile, our holiday was turning into a never-to-be-forgotten disaster.

The crunch came towards the end of the second week, when we went to see the cattle market at Taunton. Lizzy, for once, was behaving quite well and had earned three stars on the ladder which was painted in bright colours on a paper poster (behavioural modification chart, Chris called it, but only because he was doing a part-time course in psychology at the time). Anyway, three stars meant a small treat, and we duly found a pub with a lovely little garden where the girls could have a Coke and a bag of cheese and onion crisps, Lizzy's idea of ambrosia.

'I'm going to sit with Daddy Chris,' said Lizzy firmly, as she eyed the two seater benches round the table.

'No, I am!' snapped Helen, and the two began to argue. But Chris, who was usually very patient and indulgent with them, said tersely,

'I'm sitting here, next to Mummy. You two sit down and be quiet, or there'll be no crisps.' He put his arm around me – it had been a long time since he had done that – and I found myself waiting for Lizzy's first scream. But Chris, who had clearly run out of tolerance, had not finished. As Lizzy's very curls seemed to stiffen, ready for the fight, he said calmly, 'And if there's any nonsense from you, Lizzy, I'm going to spank your bottom – very hard.' He looked at her intently. 'Understand?'

Lizzy's answering wail was cut off in mid flow as Chris half-rose from his seat to carry out his threat. She was sulky, but silent. It seemed we had cracked it. Lizzy's tantrums were easier to deal with after that; we simply had to threaten her. It was peace, but at a horrible price for us. We have always been quite strict as parents, but both abhor hitting children, always a more difficult question anyway when you are looking after other people's. Helen was smacked only as a last resort and very rarely. Ruling by force and threat was alien and uncomfortable, but it taught us a valuable lesson. Our methods, which worked so well with Helen who had never known anything else, were just inappropriate for a child who expected to be smacked whenever she stepped out of line. Lizzy would be returning to just that environment. In our attempts to love and accept her, treating her just the same as our own child, we were actually making her confused and insecure. This is a problem for foster parents that to this day I have no real answer for.

I could not bring myself to hit Lizzy for wetting the bed, although her mother strongly urged me to do this when I took Lizzy to visit her. But whenever a tantrum was imminent I would raise my hand as if to strike, and there would be no more. I was not proud of this new technique. It worked, though. And only a part of me was destroyed. When Lizzy left, and I realised she had gone for good, I cried. With relief. After eight months I could stop feeling faintly disgusted with myself and put away, in a mental cupboard, all that guilt at presuming to be a mother to a child I had no real feeling for. Only long afterwards, when I reluctantly shared my woe with other, more experienced foster parents, did I see how common this can be, and it made me feel a bit better. It made me wish, also, that I had not had to discover this particular pitfall myself. I approached the next placement with more than usual trepidation.

4

'I Dunno'

Our experience with Lizzy had not been the unqualified success we may have hoped for, but we had pulled through it. We now knew a bit more about the pitfalls. We would do better next time. Inexperience made us inept at dealing with some situations; that could hardly be avoided in the early days of 'learning the ropes'. We had our health and strength, and a good deal of enthusiasm, so we looked forward to a new challenge. Within a week of Lizzy's departure, we had agreed to take on our first long-term teenager.

Roger was thirteen, again outside our five-to-nine age group. Indeed, after Nadia and Glenroy we didn't have any children of that age for years. Even when we changed our age guidelines, Social Services had an uncanny knack of finding someone just outside them. After some time, we decided to make it official, and said we would take any child between one and sixteen years old. 'That'll fix 'em,' said Chris. The very next placement was a two-month-old baby, followed by a seventeen-year-old girl.

Roger and his two older sisters had been removed from home under a Place of Safety Order. Their mother, an alcoholic, was no longer in control of herself or her family. Finally a scene between the eldest daughter and her mother ended in violence, and all the children were taken into care. Of the father there was no trace.

The girls had opted for a children's home, for the relatively short time they would be in care. Roger had expressed an interest in moving into a family. And so it was that he arrived on our doorstep, nervously erect and defiant in brand new jeans and skinhead haircut.

Roger was very small and light for his age, and the severe haircut did not entirely offset the baby roundness of his face.

There was about him a curious aura which was simultaneously pathetic and proud: a cloak of 'Don't give a toss', thrown off now and then by a sheepish grin, or a badly bitten finger nail creeping towards his mouth.

Roger refused the statutory tea or coffee and sat silent as David, his social worker, introduced us.

'I expect Roger will be wanting to see his sisters quite regularly. They're at Greenlawns, not far from here.' He turned to Roger. 'Shall I look up the phone number for you?'

Roger shrugged non-committally.

'You do *want* to see Carol and Jean?' asked David.

Again, the Shrug. 'Dunno,' Roger said, clearly determined to give nothing away.

'Well, I guess there's plenty of time to sort all that out,' I said gently. 'On to more important things. Which football team do you support?'

'I don't.'

'What, none at all?' I prompted. 'David here told us you were mad keen on football. Chris was very pleased. He's a Fulham fan himself, aren't you, Chris?'

'That's right. Maybe you and I can see a few matches together.'

'Dunno.'

I had never met a young football fanatic who wasn't desperate to tell you, bending your ear for a full hour, not only *who* they supported, but exactly why their football team was the best in the land. So I was mystified.

'You do *like* football though?' I smiled encouragingly.

'Na, not really.'

David fidgeted uncomfortably as my eyes rested on him. 'You wrote it on that form I gave you, Roger . . .'

Roger gave David a pained look. 'I 'ad to write summat. *You* said I gotta have a "interest". "What about football?" you said. So I *put* football.'

'I see. So, what *is* your hobby, then? What are you interested in?' asked Chris.

'Nuffin'.'

None of us really knew where to go next. Simultaneously, three adults raised their coffee cups and sipped. Roger stroked the cat; Helen, mercifully, was at a friend's house. There was a strained silence.

I Dunno

'Hmm. What about schools?' I asked. 'Will Roger be carrying on at his old school?'

'No,' said David. 'We have talked that one over very carefully. Roger is keen to make a clean break from his old home and start afresh, so we'll need to find a school place. Somewhere within reasonable travelling distance; he wants to be able to join school clubs and so on.'

I looked at Roger with new respect. I could hardly believe this monosyllabic lad could have contributed whole sentences to the discussion of his future. No, I was being unfair. It was, after all, a very difficult situation for a boy of his age, coming in to a family of strangers. He would open out in time, no doubt.

'Do you know any of the schools round here?' I asked.

'Nope.'

'What sort of school would you like?' asked Chris. 'You know, large or small, single-sex, mixed . . .'

'Dunno.' Shrug.

'What's your favourite subject, Roger?' asked David.

As he opened his mouth, Roger caught my eye, and we answered together. 'Dunno!' I laughed, and Roger flashed me a sheepish smile.

He was painfully shy underneath the apparent sullenness. What an ordeal all this must be for him. Torn unceremoniously from his home, bewildered and alone, he was now plonked in front of an audience of strangers for interrogation.

'Poor Roger,' I said lightly, with what I hoped was a conspiratorial grin. 'Why should he have to tell us all about himself? We'll get to know each other soon enough, won't we?'

The talk turned, inevitably in England, to the weather, and Roger gratefully took a back seat in our discussions. It was decided, with a shrug and then a grudging nod of assent from Roger, that Chris and I would approach a few schools and then help Roger make a choice between them.

In the event, it turned out to be a choice of one. It was the year of The Glut: butter, apples and, apparently, thirteen-year-old boys were in abundance. One by one, the schools we contacted regretfully informed us there was just no room for Roger.

Finally we came up with a school which had a place available. It was further away than we had hoped for, but at least they could give him a place. An interview was arranged 'so we can look each other over before finally committing ourselves,' said a cheery voice at the other end of the line. It did not sound over-encouraging.

The interview was fixed for the following Tuesday, which gave us almost a week with Roger at home, time to settle him in for what looked like a very long stay. Once he had got the measure of us, Roger became more relaxed and almost friendly. He and Helen got along famously, as most teenagers in care do with little ones. I suppose it's the opportunity to behave like a real kid under the guise of humouring a bored toddler. Many of those who come into care in their teens have missed out on childhood in one way or another. Whatever his own experience had been, Roger was making up for lost time when he romped around pretending to be Helen's horse, or crept behind the sofa, leaving the toe cap of his boot visible so that she could find him easily.

Chris and Roger played football together. I taught him to make jam tarts and promised he could have a go at making Sunday tea. Gradually, Roger opened out and became almost chatty. He shared with us his plans for going to live abroad some day; he also confided that he was not too keen on the idea of having to take a bus and train to school every day.

'Never mind,' I said cheerfully. 'At least you won't have to go back to the old school and face everyone there. And it's not that far really – you'll get used to it.'

If they take you, I added silently as I looked at the pinched, sour little face.

Roger did not seem to take his jeans off at all, even for sleep as far as I could make out. I wondered what would happen when they needed a wash. He possessed practically nothing except the clothes he stood up in: the treasured jeans, two Ben Sherman shirts, Doc Martin boots, and who-knew-what underneath. David had told me Roger would need new clothes and had arranged a clothing grant. But I didn't know how to broach the subject. I had asked Roger whether he wanted some money to go out and buy 'socks and things' but met only the inevitable shrug and a 'dunno'. Would he like *me* to buy some stuff when I went out shopping? A Shrug, and then 'Dun . . . yeah, all right.'

Not exactly fired by this enthusiasm I bought half a dozen pairs of socks and pants. Nothing had appeared in the washing basket yet. Chris would have to give Roger some sort of man-to-man talk on hygiene, I decided.

Whenever I was not too sure what to do, I always managed to find a reason why it should be Chris's responsibility anyway. This time it was simple. Personally, I shuddered at the thought of wearing the same undies for four or five days but who knows? maybe for teenage boys it was different. I knew nothing about teenage boys; at least Chris had been one, once.

One thing was clear, even to me. Roger would have to buy a new pair of trousers for his interview. He could not turn up in his jeans.

'Why not?' he asked, when I put this to him.

'Roger, it just doesn't create a very good impression, you know? I mean you look sort of . . . tough, like a skinhead.'

'Yeah?' He beamed proudly.

'But headmasters tend not to be exactly overjoyed at the thought of skinheads joining their Second Form,' I reasoned as patiently as I could. 'So we'll have to get some new trousers, a new shirt perhaps . . .'

'Na.'

'Yes.'

'I don't want trousers. I ain't going out for 'em.'

'Then you ain't getting no pocket money, Roger.'

'You can't! Says in those forms you signed you gotta give me pocket money.'

I shrugged. 'Let them fire me, then. I'll tell you this much – no co-operation, no pocket money.'

Roger looked at me with the full force of adolescent contempt for one who would stoop so low. Then he sighed. 'All right. Can I put the telly on?'

The tough shell, as we were beginning to see, was little more than protective veneer.

I felt quite proud of myself as I sauntered down the High Street the next day with Roger in tow. Calm, reasonable discussion – and a small threat to the pocket – had prevailed. Roger could see I was not to be messed about. As we peered into windows, Roger shaking his head and suggesting we try further on, I was bathed in a glow of magnanimity. We would stop for coffee somewhere as a treat.

We had almost reached the end of the High Street. There was only one shop left, a sort of jean boutique. But I was ready for that. I knew they sold corduroy trousers.

Swiftly, I guided Roger's elbow inside and with a determined gaeity steered him to a rack of suitable looking garments.

'Right,' I said.

'Right, what?'

'Which ones do you want to try on?'

'*Try on?*' He was aghast.

'Of course you've got to try them on,' I said incredulously.

'Na.'

'Roger, don't start any nonsense now.'

A mulish look settled on the thin face. 'Ain't trying nuffin *on*.'

I decided to try and sidestep the issue. Perhaps we could change them if they were the wrong size.

'Which colour would you like? Black? Grey? What?'

'None of them.'

I drew a deep breath and pasted a tolerant smile over my teeth.

'Black would look nice. Match your boots – and your expression. What size?'

'Size?'

One two, three, I counted.

'Yes, size, Roger. Waist, inside leg – you know, like "30–32" Which size do you wear?'

'Dunno.'

Four, five. We would not be stopping for that coffee. I picked a pair off the rack at random. 'It looks like you'll have to try some on, then, to give us an idea. Come on.'

'Said I don't want to.'

'I did not ask if you wanted to,' I pointed out. I was aware of a hopeful-looking assistant bearing down upon us, and I began to feel very conspicuous. 'Roger, just do it. Please.'

'Na.' He looked me straight in the eye. 'I ain't tryin' them on. I'll 'ave to undo the laces on me boots!'

Six, seven, eight. It was no good. I was going to clobber the little . . .

'May I help you, Madam?'

'I'm not sure,' I smiled sweetly, mentally pleading for a thunderbolt, just a small one, to fall on Roger. 'My . . . er, the lad here needs some trousers. But he doesn't know the size.'

'I'll get a tape measure.'

'No!' Clearly horrified at the thought of a stranger's hand creeping up his inside leg, Roger stepped back into the rack, pulling several pairs of trousers onto the floor.

'Roger, there is no point in buying trousers if you don't know the size. We would only have to bring them back and go through this whole fiasco again.'

'Don't buy 'em, then, I'll go in me jeans.'

'You're behaving like a baby!' I snapped. 'A little brat!' We were beginning to attract an audience. The assistant, embarrassed, muttered, 'Um, look, I'll just go and . . . do call if you need help.' He disappeared, no doubt to watch from a safe distance and open a book on the outcome.

I took a pair of black cord trousers off the rail and handed them to Roger. He did not move. I held them against his middle; the legs were too long, but the waist looked about right. Without a word, I headed for the cash desk.

'We'll take these,' I said airily. As soon as the money had been paid and the trousers handed over, I dashed for the door. Roger followed me out. I threw the bag at him, wishing there was a brick buried in it.

'That's that done, then. Now listen carefully. When we get home, you will put those on and I will turn them up. Tomorrow, you *will* wear them to your interview; after that, you can shred them with the garden shears for all I care – it's *your* clothing allowance.'

Expecting more argument, I was already phrasing a scorchingly

sarcastic offer to help him tie his bootlaces after the great ordeal. I almost missed the quiet, 'O.K. Only . . .'

I stopped dead on the busy High Street, looked briefly heavenward and then at Roger. 'Only *what*, Roger?'

He gave me a half-smile. 'I wanted grey, really.'

The following morning Chris, Roger and I dropped Helen at nursery school and went straight on to the interview. The school was a large, modern complex in a fashionable district. The street was quiet and leafy, and the school appeared to have very large grounds for its location. Our first impression was quite favourable. The graffiti was considerately positioned so that you were well inside before you even saw it.

We sat outside the Secretary's office in a row, like three little monkeys. Finally a huge, genial-looking man appeared. He wore traditional teachers' garb straight out of a *Guardian* cartoon: bulging pockets in a slightly shabby tweed jacket, dark trousers and a stringy-looking tie. He pulled each of us to our feet in turn with a firm, chalky handshake.

'I'm Colin Haydn,' he said, beaming from ear to ear. 'I'll be the Form Tutor for Roger, if he comes here. Good to see you – follow me.'

We went with him through a maze of corridors, across a playground and up some stairs. As we passed the boys' loo, two girls shot out, holding on to each other and screaming with laughter.

'F—ing little cows!' An irate male pupil followed them out. He did not bat an eye-lid when he saw us. The girls minced away.

'All right?' beamed Haydn. The boy opened his mouth to reply. 'Good, good – now, off we go, eh?'

And he strolled on. Chris and I raised eyebrows at each other. Roger, catching the exchange, grinned.

'We're going to see John Henderson, Head of Second Year,' explained Haydn. 'Just a formality, I hope. Tell you about ourselves, see if we're suited.' He patted Roger on the shoulder and dodged to one side as a crowd of pupils shoved and jostled us on their way down the corridor. The language was . . . colourful.

'Now, now,' Haydn's great beam never wavered for an instant. He pointed to us. 'Visitors, you know . . .'

The group looked singularly unimpressed.

As Haydn and Roger strode on ahead, I hissed, 'I don't think so, do you? Let's get away as soon as we can.'

'We've got no choice, remember?' whispered Chris in turn. 'Anyway, I don't expect it's as bad as it looks.'

I decided to reserve judgement on that one; I had serious doubts about the disciplinary power of 'Now, now, Visitors . . .' I wondered how many teachers were at this very moment climbing the walls of their classrooms looking for escape.

At last we arrived at the Head of Year's office in the bowels of the building. When he rose from his chair to greet us I did not miss Roger's triumphant smile. Mr John Henderson was wearing jeans; jeans that were far more faded and in need of repair than those I had torn from Roger.

Perhaps we were simply victims to an unfortunate beginning. Perhaps I am simply a closet fascist who wants to see all the individuality beaten out of the next generation. But the interview was doomed from the start as far as I was concerned. We listened

in astonishment as Haydn and Henderson expounded their joint
theories of education.

The very ethos of the school was Informality, the Family
Atmosphere. The aim was to provide a Receptive Environment,
where pupils could develop as Whole Beings and reach their own
Fulfillment, developing their Individual Potential to the full. This
pair should be selling clichés door to door, I felt.

In keeping with this rather radical approach, they continued, all
teachers were known to the pupils by their Christian names. The
school had no uniform, and the curriculum was worked out after
Full Consultation with the student body.

'Exams?' I queried hesitantly.

Mr Henderson – John – leaned back in his chair with the air of
one who was quite accustomed to dealing with *this* sort of parent.

'Examinations have their place, of course. We do the full range
of 'O' and 'A' level subjects. But exams are not the be-all and
end-all of our existence. We believe academic success is not as
important as being a Whole Person, equipped to deal with the
demands of a Modern Society.'

I wondered how many of his Whole People, whole that is except
for qualifications, would be seeking their Full Potential outside
the Labour Exchange, in years to come.

Chris had said nothing. His expression was one of intense
interest. This was a clear danger signal. The look was one I knew
particularly well. Chris was forming his verbal battle lines. It was
time to leave before he mounted the assault. I rose to my feet.

'Thank you very much for seeing us, Mr. . . . John, Colin.'

'Not at all. We have a place here for Roger as soon as you like.
Are you off to see any more schools?'

'Um . . .no. No, this is the only one,' I stumbled grudgingly.

'Right, well, no sense in wasting any more of a valuable term
time, eh? Bring Roger tomorrow – we'll complete the paperwork
then.'

And that, admittedly with sinking hearts, is what we did.

As he settled into school, Roger became much more one of the
family. He was, in many ways, a very difficult child, and we had
many blazing rows. There was a great chip on Roger's shoulder
which weighed him down. He hated his mother, and was full of
scorn for the father who had cleared off and left him. Chris and I
had to bear the brunt of this, as well as the usual teenage troubles

any parent has to endure.

I used to think we were very disadvantaged in this sort of situation, not having older children of our own to give us experience in 'handling' teenagers. But now, as I look back over the various placements, I see it differently. We were not tied to these children by any bonds of birth, love, guilt – all the usual threads woven into the pattern of parenting. If the kids turned out 'wrong', no-one was going to say it was our fault. We could be more objective, plan strategies, even laugh a lot more easily over other people's children than we could our own.

Yet Roger became, in our minds, very close to being 'ours'. We *felt* like his parents, and sometimes actually forgot that we weren't. This was ludicrous, because we were far too young, in our mid-twenties, for it to be even a biological possibility.

We looked forward to seeing Roger grow up and perhaps marry, have children of his own. There was even a bit of talk with his Social Worker about possible adoption.

Roger, as far as he was able to talk about matters so close to his heart, was desolate at being without a family of his own. I assured him he was very much welcome in ours. Shyly, he even asked me if he could call us Mum and Dad, like Helen. This, from a by-now fourteen-year-old toughie, brought a lump to my throat.

I almost told Roger that we were thinking of adoption, there and then. But we could not be sure it would all go through, or that we were even committed enough. I said nothing, simply nodded and tried to cover his blushes with an embarrassed hug. The moment passed, and was all but forgotten. It was just as well: I had reason to be grateful for my silence, later on.

5

Foster Gran

By the time he had been with us for six months or so, Roger had
slotted in to the family very well. He was still no conversationalist,
and still had terrible black moods which were difficult to shift. We
had not given up the idea of adopting Roger, but numerous
practical difficulties were making us very cautious, and we had
done little more than talk about the possibility together. In the
meantime, we had been joined by Julie, dubbed 'the clockwork
baby' because she was so easy to look after.

Julie was not really a baby at all; she was almost two years old.
She was a rosy-cheeked, chubby little cherub in a permanent state
of cheerfulness, and we all loved her on sight. Even Roger allowed
her onto his lap and submitted, blushing, to her generous kisses.

Julie's mother, in contrast, was suffering severe post-natal
depression after the birth of a second child. Since Julie's father
was also ill, Julie was staying with us until something was worked
out at home.

Life was running very smoothly, more of a quiet stream than a
rushing river. So I should have known we were about to hit
Niagara. It was about this time we first heard of Karen.

Our own link worker, Neil, was coincidentally the Social
Worker responsible for Karen, too. He approached us with some
hesitancy about Karen but he knew us well by this time, and felt
we were the right people. Or at least, he was desperate and the
Muggins Millers were the only available alternative.

Karen was fifteen years old and pregnant. This may have
seemed enough of a problem, but there was more. Karen was
actually already in care, and living in a children's home. She and
her boyfriend were very keen to have – and keep – the baby, but
there was no possibility of Karen staying on in the children's

home. The baby was due in three months time, and strenuous efforts to find somewhere for mother and child to go had turned up only one option, a mother and baby unit in Hertfordshire. Karen was apparently set against this idea. We also felt it was inappropriate for someone so young and so vulnerable. The question was, could *we* take her on?

There were immediate practical difficulties. Our house had four large bedrooms, but one had been converted into a study/family room and was not equipped to take a mother and child. The other three rooms were occupied. Clearly Karen could not share with Roger, or us. It would mean moving Julie from Helen's room into ours.

'She would have to share with Helen,' I told Neil doubtfully. 'And the baby too, when it arrives. The room's not *that* big. I'm not sure it's fair to Helen or to Karen.'

'I know there would be enormous practical difficulties on that score, Beth. But if you could take her just until the baby is born, it would help. It would give us a bit more time – we could decide what to do next later.'

I was surprised at Neil not wanting everything cut and dried at the outset. He really must be desperate. Still, I could not readily agree to put the whole family through that sort of upheaval.

'Look, Neil, I just don't know. Let me talk to Chris and the kids. Call me back later this afternoon if you still haven't found anything better, O.K.?' It was the best I could do.

Chris immediately expressed the same doubts as me. 'We really don't have room, do we?'

As we talked it over, though, the idea did not seem impossible. We could just about manage, at least until the baby was born. That would give us the opportunity to get to know Karen, support her through the birth. If things went well, we could at least maintain a link and be on hand to help, even if she was not living with us.

Finally, we decided to leave it all in the hands of the children: Roger, Helen and Karen. Julie, of course, was too young to consult. If they went for the idea in spite of the difficulties, we would go ahead.

Helen, who thrived on change and commotion, waved aside any suggestion of inconvenience. She was too young to understand the long-term implications, and was thrilled with the whole idea. I had to restrain her from going upstairs to clear out drawers and cupboards on the spot. Roger spent a lot of time exclaiming over the possibility of being pregnant at fifteen. I narrowed my eyes at him suspiciously, but he seemed, to my astonishment, to have a serious gap somewhere in his knowledge. Another job for Chris.

'A little baby would be neat,' said Roger finally. A whole sentence from Roger was always a mark of strong feeling.

When Neil telephoned again, I asked him to explain the problems of space very carefully to Karen, and bring her round to see us. I still felt doubtful, but in the back of my mind I knew that even this would be better than starting a new life and a new experience of motherhood in an institution, far removed from the family life of which a birth should mark the beginning.

Not once did the inevitable moral questions in all this occur to us. In fact we were surprised, and a little annoyed, when someone asked us if we had any problems 'with our faith' in harbouring an under-age unmarried mother. It has cropped up several times since, and still leaves me with a vague feeling of surprise. It seems God, who loves all and forgives all, makes an exception in the case of any sin tainted with you-know-what. There was a child, about to bring another child into the world. Any mother and father worth their salt would respond. That was all we saw.

Karen duly arrived for a preliminary visit. She was petite, attractive and as cool as a cucumber. Only a slight flicker in her eyes now and then betrayed any apprehension. She was trying, with some success, to appear much older than her fifteen years, and very sophisticated. I asked how she thought she'd cope, with a new baby. Karen held out a hand to steady Julie, who was trying to clamber on to her lap.

'Oh, I've already brought up babies,' she answered calmly.

Neil explained that Karen was the eldest of a large family.

'So you're an experienced mother already?' said Chris. 'Then perhaps you can pass on a few tips to Beth here.'

Karen smiled. The ice was broken. Together we all trooped upstairs to inspect Helen's bedroom. Proudly she showed Karen the drawers and cupboards she had emptied, and the Mickey Mouse sticker she had put by to give the baby, when it came. Helen was very taken with Karen from the beginning and Karen, quite naturally, took her by the hand.

'Wouldn't you mind me being here, Helen? I might wake you up at night.'

Helen shook her head.

'If you wake *me* up, I'll just go and wake Mummy and Daddy up. *They'll* play with me until I can get back to sleep.'

So, she had been ahead of us all on this one. I wondered what else the little schemer had worked out.

'What do you think?' Neil asked Karen when we were downstairs again. She shook her head slowly; her words surprised us all.

'I don't want to go to the mother and baby unit,' she said. 'But I don't want to make life hard for everybody else, either.'

I was touched by the maturity and selflessness of her response. Karen needed a place, not just a physical space to live in but a real place in someone's life, somewhere safe. I leaned towards her and took her hand.

'Karen, look. If you come, it'll be hard – very hard, I expect. There'll be times when we're all yelling at each other and moaning about sharing rooms and what-have-you. We can't even guarantee it'll work out once the baby is born. But if we weren't all willing to give it a try, well, you wouldn't be here, would you?'

Karen's dark, troubled eyes travelled over to Chris and then settled on mine. 'What do *you* think?' she asked.

'Oh, *we* want you to come,' I said at once. 'Anyone can be a foster-mum, after all. But who could pass up the opportunity of being a foster-*gran*?'

As she left, Karen hugged both Chris and me. We had arranged for her to spend the following weekend with us. If this went smoothly, Karen would move in with us the following week.

Like many a best-laid scheme, however, this one was to gang aft agley – and soon. Two days later, Neil telephoned.

'Prepare yourself,' he said. 'Karen won't be coming this weekend.'

'Oh.' Despite our apprehension, I realised I was disappointed. 'What's up?'

'She's had the baby – they're in hospital.'

'Are they all right? I mean, did the baby . . .?'

I was frantically trying to work out how premature it was.

'They're both well. The baby – a girl, by the way, was nearly twelve weeks early, but they say her lungs are far better than could be hoped for. She weighs just over four pounds. Looks like she'll pull through.'

'And Karen? How's Karen?'

'A bit shocked by it all, I think, but quite chirpy when I saw her. Physically, she's very fit.'

'So what happens now? I mean, we had arranged for her to stay until the birth.'

'I know, Beth. We need to talk about that. The baby in any case will be in hospital for some time. Let me give you all the details and then you can visit, if you want to.'

'Of course we want to, don't be daft.'

Our first sight of Tina was through the thick, impersonal glass of the special baby unit. She lay in her mother's arms like a new-born gerbil, pink and wriggly. That was the only impression I could form from that distance. Karen seemed quite at ease in handling her, and her face shone with maternal pride as she held Tina closer to the glass.

It was here, too, that we met Wayne for the first time. We liked him very much. He was affable, happy-go-lucky, and genuinely besotted with Karen. He called her his 'wife'.

As I watched them together with their infant daughter I could not ignore a spasm of anxiety. They were playing a game, a very sophisticated version of mothers and fathers, but a game nonetheless. They were supremely confident, invincible, and would conquer all.

For a moment I was reminded of Helen, soon after she learned to walk. I was cleaning upstairs, and suddenly noticed her heading for the top of stairs. She prepared to step over the edge with not a single thought for the consequences; I caught her not a second too soon. I hoped *this* little family could be saved from trying the stairs too soon.

Glum thoughts for such a happy occasion. I shoved them aside and joined in the exclamations and the general jollity.

'Look,' Karen patted her stomach. 'Flat as a board.' It was, too – her figure had sprung back to slenderness like a released spring.

Wayne drew Chris to one side. 'When Karen comes to stay, is it all right to visit her, after work and that?'

'Of course,' I heard Chris say. 'Any time you like. In fact, the more time you spend together the better.'

It was then that I realised no-one had even thought about cancelling the placement. We all just naturally carried on.

The strength of the bond we formed with Karen was unique in all our experience of fostering. Perhaps it was the circumstances, that sharing which comes about with the birth of a baby. Perhaps it was Karen's youth and vulnerability that made us want to protect her, and her child. Or perhaps it was just plain good fortune that the sort of teenage daughter we would be delighted to have (premature parenthood excepted) was virtually delivered to our door.

Karen left hospital a week later; Tina had to stay behind until her weight reached five pounds and five ounces. Karen's possessions were moved from the children's home into Helen's room. We had already settled Julie into her new position in a cot at the end of our bed. She did not seem to mind at all, and it was a joy to see her grinning at us over the foot of the bed each morning. It did feel a little squeezed, though. I had serious doubts about adding baby Tina to the clutter Helen and Karen had already managed between them. Only Roger, as he would smugly remind us, had the real privacy of a room to himself. We adapted though, spurred on perhaps by my mother's accounts of the top-to-toe sardine arrangements experienced by many families when *she* were a lass. At least there was the study – we all somehow got a turn on our own in there.

Meanwhile, Karen went to the hospital every day to feed Tina and care for her, under the supervision of the Nurses. Her daily bulletins on Tina's progress were eagerly awaited by us all. Roger and Helen were most disgruntled about not being allowed into the special unit. They waited for Tina's homecoming as if it were Christmas.

The great day finally came. Tina, topping the scale at five pounds five and a half ounces, was pronounced ready to come home.

The usual celebrations followed: 'what tiny hands . . . oh, let's see her toes . . . she just smiled at me – it *was* a smile . . . ugh!' That sort of thing. Tina was tiny, and beautiful, and we were all entranced. Julie beamed from ear to ear, and tried to poke Tina in the eye as her own special welcoming gesture.

Karen and Wayne, although still almost children themselves, were typical proud parents. Karen busied herself in old parentcraft magazines that I had kept. Wayne was fondly told off for 'spoiling' Tina, and was even occasionally found poking her when she was asleep, so that he could cuddle her back to sleep again.

Those first few weeks were wonderful. We were all carried along on a euphoric bandwagon, heading for the credits and a glorious sunset. Our house was full, or so we thought, and everyone was knitting together with a real community spirit. The atmosphere was almost festive, party-like. We only needed a final, zany garnish. And even that was in the pipeline.

6

Glen Rules – O.K.?

There were times as a foster mother when I could almost feel a cosy 'Earth Mother' glow surrounding me like a warm halo of sunshine. On such days I wore an apron, and baked vast batches of peanut butter cookies. I promised nature rambles or finger painting, and envisaged my scrubbed, rosy-cheeked little charges snuggling down, heavy-eyed and soporific, while I told them gentle tales of pumpkin carriages and sleeping princesses.

The day of Glen's arrival had been such a day, at first, but had backfired – as it usually did. Helen had a couple of friends over to play. Julie was having a wonderful time being fussed over, and the children were very patient with her attempts to join their game. It gave me some peace, and I promised an outing when I had finished my baking. But the children were not terribly thrilled at the idea of a nature ramble. They wanted to go to the park, where there were swings and slides, and an ice cream stand. Blow number one.

There was not enough peanut butter for a full batch of cookies, and a special trip to the supermarket served only to prove Whatsisname's Law that everyday items are only in abundance when you have no particular need of them. Undaunted, I embarked upon home-made caraway bread *and* quiche *and* ginger snaps, with visions of a fragrant farmhouse tea in our leafless, pollution-surrounded city house.

Once all the mixing was done, at the point of no return, I suddenly lost enthusiasm. I didn't feel cosy, I felt knackered. The children appeared from the garden, having finished building their worm sanctuary with my slotted spoon. 'And the children', Helen informed me solemnly, 'want to help with the baking,' which seemed the last straw.

Through clenched teeth, I smilingly pointed out that the sooner
I was finished, the sooner we could be at the park (Oh, how my
aching legs regretted that suggestion), and their 'help' did tend to
make me a *teeny* bit slower. Anyway, I said desperately, *Play-
school* was about to start. Instant success. The very mention of the
beloved television left me once more alone. Sighing, I pushed my
arms into the bread dough.

The phone rang.

Damn them, I thought fiercely, they could call back later. I
carried on punching the dough with a savage relish.

'Mummy – the phone's ringing.' Helen's head was poking round
the door.

'I know.'

Helen was climbing onto a chair. 'I can answer it.'

'No, it's all right – *don't*!'

'Hallo? My name's Helen. Do you want my Mummy? Here she
is.'

Helen held the phone out to me. After watching me trying to
disentangle my clogged fingers for a moment, she put the phone
down on the top of the rolled out quiche pastry and left the room.

With the awful knowledge that this whole day had been a
mistake, I lunged for the earpiece before the lead, stretched to its
maximum, snatched it back to the wall socket.

'Hallo?' It was a social worker. I might have known.

This one's name was Mary. I knew her slightly from the local
foster parents' support group. She wanted to know if we could take
seventeen-year-old Glen that night. Boarding school had closed
down for the summer, and his usual foster mother was ill in
hospital.

Mary told me that Glen was disabled – he had been born without
legs. His mother had rejected him very early on and his unmarried
parents had split up. Glen had been in care virtually all his life.

'Oh, Mary, I don't know.' I rubbed my hand over my apron to
get rid of the worst of the dough lumps, and swapped the receiver
to my other ear. 'Everything's so hectic here at the moment.'

But I knew, and Mary knew, that I was not going to say an
outright 'no'. We were not yet experienced enough. It took us two
years of non-stop short term placements before we discovered how
to say no, and mean it – and not feel guilty afterwards.

'It's just for a week or so,' Mary was reassuring. Well, a week was nothing. It was the 'or so' bit I didn't like.

'Yes, all right then. We'll give it a go. I'm just a bit worried about how the others will react.'

Glen would make six children in all, I mentally counted. (We seemed always to be counting our children, never sure that one had not been secretly added.) We had fifteen-year-old Karen, thirteen-year-old Roger and the 'littlies' – Julie, baby Tina and our own Helen, all in various stages from the feeding one's nose stage to the what-fun-to-play-with-Mummy's-make-up stage. I reflected ruefully that one more person couldn't mean any more chaos, and at least there was no space left. So we couldn't take another child, even if we wanted to (I had a lot to learn).

Mary was telephoning from Sussex, from an area office near to the school. She would collect Glen and bring him to us in the early evening. Replacing the phone and absentmindedly wiping it with my doughy apron, I groaned inwardly at the thought of the baking, the park, the telling of the news to the gathered hordes at tea-time. I knew Roger would not want anyone 'Weird' sleeping in the spare bed in his room, and I knew the children would all roll about cracking awful boy-with-no-legs jokes. My brood, en masse, had as much sensitivity between them as a packet of thawed fish fingers. I knew they could be counted on to keep their mouths shut once Glen arrived, but I already felt a warm flush of embarrassment at the thought of their probing stares.

After telephoning Chris and extracting a generous promise to get home early if he could, I went back to my chores with a sense of hopeless resignation. Later on, tea having been as riotous as I had gloomily anticipated, there was another call from Mary. She was on her way from Sussex with Glen, but had discovered something from the staff at his school that she thought we ought to know. My heart fell right into my Earth Mother Hush Puppies.

Glen had been thrown out of the local disco and banned forever for – wait for it – biting girls' legs.

'What?' was all I could say at first. I thought of Karen, our slender, vivacious and leggy fifteen-year-old, and closed my eyes as Mary said yes, I had heard correctly, and told the full story.

Glen had always refused to wear his artificial legs and looked rather . . . odd. When a couple of local lasses had tittered together, Glen had taken it as a calculated insult and gone for their legs.

My eyes still firmly closed – since I was surely daydreaming, it seemed only right – I began to stutter: 'I'm sorry, Mary, but I don't think . . .'

'Please, Beth.' She sounded a tinge desperate. 'I've absolutely nowhere else to take him. Just for tonight. See how it goes. Please.'

I gritted my teeth, muttered 'O.K.' and put the phone down before I had thought to ask her why *she* couldn't take him home with her.

Chris, all expectant, was waiting for news, having been intrigued by my end of the conversation.

'Why can't *she* take him home?' were his first words when I told him.

'Social Workers cannot afford to become involved with their Clients,' I said primly, peering at him over the top of my specs, still dusted with flour.

We laughed together, grimly, and decided not to tell Karen about this latest development. She wore jeans most of the time anyway.

Eventually, late that night, Glen arrived. He stood about three-and-a-half feet tall in his leather Hells Angel jacket and walked on his hands, gorilla-style. Mary came two steps behind him, carrying his artificial legs.

Understandably nervous, we all sat on the edge of our seats drinking tea and making polite conversation. The kids were all in bed, except for Karen, who could not be dragged away from the late-night film but would undoubtedly burst in at any moment.

'Well Glen,' I said. 'What do you do, you know, for a hobby . . . or whatever?'

'I kill skinheads.'

I laughed nervously, meeting Chris's startled blue eyes. 'Oh, do you?'

'Yeah. I hate 'em.'

My fears for Karen's legs were immediately supplanted by my anxiety for Roger. At this very moment, Roger's close-cropped head lay on a pillow in the room he was to share with Glen. Laid out on a chair beneath his 'Madness' posters were his jeans, 'Doc Martin's' and Ben Sherman shirt, all neatly pressed ready for school.

'Ah. Well, I hope you will restrain yourself. In the house at least. Er . . . you're sharing a room with one.' I smiled very brightly.

'You'll have to hold me back then,' came the reply.

While the social worker hurriedly gathered her things together to make a quick dash for it, Glen told us that his friend, who was confined to a wheelchair, had been attacked by a group of skinheads. Turfing him out of his wheelchair, they left him lying helpless on the pavement. Glen shuddered at the memory of his friend's pain and humiliation, and then shrugged.

'He wasn't able to defend himself. Well *I* can, and it's my business to get 'em – get 'em all!'

I swallowed. Chris looked very pale. We looked at Glen's massive biceps, developed through years of swinging his body weight on his hands. And we looked at each other, feeling any control of the situation slipping away from us.

'Surely, Glen, with you being so short, they only have to kick you in the head,' began Chris.

Glen gestured impatiently.

'They kick at me, I grab their leg and pull 'em to the floor, and it's all over.'

You needed only to look at him to know that this was true. Glen's torso and arms were those of a heavyweight boxer. Seated at a table, he looked about seven feet tall – Superman's stand-in for all the aggro scenes. We went to bed that night with heavy hearts.

In the end, however, Glen stayed about two weeks and was perhaps the least trouble of all our older foster children. He slept late and was out until midnight most days.

Helen met his legs long before she met him. They were left in the hallway; Glen found them uncomfortable but kept them 'just in case', and Helen was fascinated by them. She would walk them down the hall, tenderly cooing, 'Come along now, Mr Jones, that's right. Good – GOOD,' in her best nurse's voice. I never quite figured out what was wrong with Mr Jones; probably he had the opposite problem to Glen. I did not enquire. Helen, being used to a life where truth was often stranger than fiction, had a vivid imagination and made up impossibly convoluted case histories which I could not follow.

Thankfully, Glen pronounced Roger to be 'not a *real* skinhead'. (I dared Roger, with a look designed to kill at twenty paces, to argue about that.) And Karen's legs remained unmolested. In

fact, Glen was polite, independent and helpful. He was forever popping Tina's dummy back into her mouth as he passed the cradle, and was not above the occasional romp with Julie either. Glen's behaviour in the neighbourhood was also impeccable, apart from one small incident where a little skinhead from around the corner was pulled off his bike in the midst of an insulting repartee. After throwing him to the ground, muddying his jeans and de-Shermanising his shirt forever, Glen became something of a local hero. The kid, apparently, had it coming. That seemed to be the general opinion.

Glen also took the dog out for a walk every day, an amazing sight as they ran down the road together, almost the same height. They were usually followed by one or two other bemused animals trying to work out what was going on. Glen liked to be with dogs. He was not always craning up to see their faces and they made him feel, I think, truly big and masterful.

When Glen finally left we knew we were going to miss him. He certainly took some getting used to, but everyone agreed that Glen was 'all right'. He was returning to his usual foster family, where his foster mother was out of hospital and convalescing.

Glen has visited us once or twice since, and we have been glad to see him robust and unbowed as ever. Glen, although touchy about his handicap, refused to let it crush him. He was to be in our minds for many years to come, whenever Chris and I had to tackle a problem that left us despairing.

* * *

The week after Glen left we said goodbye to Julie, our clockwork cherub. She was returning home to the joint care of her mother and grandma. We would miss her, but it was lovely to see her mother looking so much better and we could only be happy for them.

So there we were, bathed in satisfaction, glorying in how smoothly we were pulling it off. We were being hopelessly optimistic. During Glen's stay, when everything had gone so well, we were experiencing a 'honeymoon' period which is common in long-term fostering. For a while, everyone is at their best, adapting to a new situation and trying with all their might to create the right impression. It is as the family reverts to its natural style, and people relax into their normal standards of behaviour, that problems occur. Chris and I had not expected anything like this. It was not until months later that we learnt even how common a situation it was, from other foster parents at a local foster-parent group. These groups, together with the regular magazine and information literature distributed by the National Foster Care Association, are an invaluable source of sympathetic support and useful knowledge. We learned much more from these over the years than we could hope to learn at the official 'training sessions'. For a month, Chris and I were telling each other how wonderful it all was. But the end of the wonderfulness was in sight.

Tina turned out to be the most miserable baby I have ever come across. She was permanently hungry, but invariably threw back whatever was given her. Karen gave up breastfeeding very early on; we were only surprised she had lasted the first week. Three or four times a night, a thin wail would rise through the darkened house, starting both Karen and I awake.

In the first few weeks it was not so bad, but as time wore on the lack of sleep took its toll on both of us. I was taking turns with Karen in getting up to Tina, but I had a house and other children to see to. I felt permanently tired.

Karen began to see Tina's behaviour as a personal vendetta. She almost believed Tina was getting at her on purpose. I could not risk going up to the top floor of the house, out of earshot, to catch up on sleep. Tina's waking cry would be followed by shouts and angry threats coming from the bedroom next door. Helen, mercifully, slept through it all with her father's night-deadness.

Scared out of my wits that something had happened, I would

fling on my dressing gown and dive into the room, always half-expecting to find a tiny battered body. I could see Karen was on the edge of catastrophe. I was too tired to think straight, even for myself. Neil was on leave and it was almost impossible to find a Social Worker at all, never mind one who knew Karen well enough to be of help.

I wanted to make it right for her; I wanted it so badly it was a real, physical ache. Chris and I started taking Tina into our room on all but two nights of the week. That did not help. It made me even more exhausted and Karen found it even more difficult to cope with Tina on the nights she did have her, now that she compared them to the blissful nights when she didn't.

Tina, sensing the tension of those who handled her, became more and more difficult to pacify, during the day as well as at night. Karen snarled at the baby whenever she moved, or made a sound. We were all locked in a vicious, ever-diminishing circle. I could not look at the situation objectively at all. Chris would come home to a family steeped in varying degrees of misery, to be instantly claimed by Helen as the only person who had time to listen to her prattle.

In the face of all this, Karen's sophistication vanished. She became depressed, touchy, longing for the teenage life she had thrown away before it ever began.

'I'm just popping out,' she would say, and be gone. Hours later she would return, having met up with some friends and spent the afternoon at the ice rink, or shopping, without a thought for Tina. Horrified, I saw her growing away from our dreams of a home of her own, marriage to Wayne and a good chance of happiness.

'What shall we do? What can we do?' I would ask myself. Chris and Neil and I conferred often, but none of us really knew how to resolve the situation. Instinctively, I wanted to take over the care of Tina entirely, giving back to Karen the freedom of a regular teenager and to Tina the love and security we knew were crucial to her well-being. Certainly, Karen would have jumped at the chance. But reason seemed to be against such a move.

'How will she *ever* learn to cope if she gives up at the start?' Chris wondered.

'And,' I added, 'What will she do if she no longer has the baby to take care of? Go back to school? Get a job? I mean, how can we have them both *here*, but not together? Life would be impossible.'

Neil put it rather more bluntly. 'If Karen gives over the care of Tina to you, then we will have to treat that as a final decision – officially, I mean. Tina would be taken into care, and fostered by you. Karen would return to the children's home or, more likely, a hostel.' (It was a curious anomaly that, although Karen was in care, Tina was not. There was no justification in law to take out a care order.) Karen and Wayne had both been so determined at the start that Tina would never, ever, have to go into care. It would surely break them to see this happening. It would be like a total, final eclipse of the sun, with no ray of hope. I could not give everything up to it, not without a fight.

In the end, we decided on one last, concentrated effort. A case conference was called. This involved Karen, Wayne, Neil and ourselves, plus a few specialists and senior Social Workers. I think everybody attending the meeting faced it with an inevitable sense of doom. But as the evening wore on and the intolerable situation was opened up and discussed, with objective opinions and guidance from those who had specialist expertise but no close involvement with the family, we all began to get a lift. By the time the meeting adjourned to the local pub a new possibility of making it work had uplifted us all.

Chris and I were to take charge of Tina with a planned, step-by-step programme to follow, whereby the tasks and re-sponsibilities would be handed back gradually. The 'carrot' was a flat for Karen and Wayne to move into the following year, if they had shown they were capable of managing.

By this time, with all the children, and the house to care for, with so little sleep, I felt like an extra-terrestrial without his life support. So it was decided that Wayne would stay with us at weekends, bedding down on the top floor, with Tina in her cot beside him. Then at least I could look forward to two undisturbed nights each week.

Everyone was happy with this arrangement. Karen looked as though she had escaped being crushed alive. Wayne, who had been a frequent visitor anyway, was no disruption. Indeed, Wayne was a perfect mother. He was calm, cheerful, completely un-flappable. Although he worked long hours, he took his two broken nights in his stride and never complained.

I have to admit I was a bit concerned about some of his

baby-care methods. When Wayne prepared feeds, I had to look the other way and trust to the mercy of God and the strength of Tina's constitution. But both Chris and I trusted him to stay calm with Tina whatever she did, and it was a weight off our minds when he was home.

At first, Karen threw herself into the routine with enthusiasm. She helped with the cleaning and shopping, cuddled and played with Tina, went out with her friends on pre-arranged outings, and cooked dinner for herself and Wayne twice a week. Everybody relaxed, and the difference in Tina was dramatic. She was by now six months old, still tiny but quite strong. Overnight, Tina became a new baby: happy, gurgling, adventurous. I felt ashamed we had not done something earlier.

'I'm sorry, Tina – so sorry,' I would whisper as I cuddled her to me. The round green eyes would stare at the tear rolling down my cheek and then crease up with laughter as she plunged her hands into my hair and pulled. For the first time in months, the future looked hopeful. Even Roger was heard to grunt, 'Baby's happy, innit?' He and Helen must have been relieved to have their fair share of attention again.

'Perhaps they will pull it off,' I would say to Chris so often he must have grown sick of it. 'Perhaps it *will* be all right after all.' I knew, though, that the cards were stacked against them. 'It *will* come right, it *must* come right,' I said, over and over. It was an incantation, a talisman against the incoming tide that, at the back of my mind, I knew could not be stopped.

Karen was enjoying her freedom. Wayne was becoming jealous of her twice-weekly jaunts to the ice rink. He was convinced Karen was seeing another boy there. Was she? What would happen if it were true?

My worries over Karen's future, however, were unexpectedly diverted one day when I opened the door to find a charming man standing there, with a broad smile and the hint of an Irish accent.

'Mrs Miller?'

'Yes.'

'Is Roger in?'

'Roger?' With a caution any foster parent will recognise, I adopted a blank expression and searched my memory. No, I hadn't seen this man before – but there was no instruction to keep Roger's whereabouts a secret.

'Roger Flaherty. Social Services told me he was here, with you.'
It must be all right, then. I opened the door wider.
'Please come in. I'll go and tell Roger you're here, Mr . . .?'
With a flashing smile, the stranger extended his hand.
'Joseph Flaherty. I'm Roger's Dad.'

7
Family Ties

I don't know who was more astonished at Joseph Flaherty's arrival on the scene, myself or Roger. After initial introductions and small talk I left the pair alone, perched uneasily on the sofa. Roger looked shell-shocked.

'Who's that man?' demanded Helen.

'That's Roger's Daddy.'

'He doesn't have a Daddy.'

'Yes, he does. And a Mummy.'

'Why is he here, then?'

This question, as always, put me at a loss. How much can you explain to a small child and still keep faith with the newcomer?

'Well,' I said, 'I really don't know. Sometimes Mummies and Daddies just can't look after their children properly, and so they ask someone else to do it. I've explained all this before, Helen. Now, shall we go and make some tea?'

'I want to go in there and listen.'

'You can't. It's private.'

She looked at me with a gleam in her eye.

'I could listen at the keyhole.'

'Helen!'

She shrugged her shoulders nonchalantly and wandered into the kitchen in search of a biscuit barrel. I decided not to ask where Helen had acquired the knack of eavesdropping, or how long she had been practising it. But when we went to bed that night I closed the door very firmly.

'Why are you whispering?' demanded Chris.

'I feel our daughter's education has gone far enough at present.' I said enigmatically, and refused to explain any further.

When I took a tray of tea in for Roger and his father, they were talking nineteen to the dozen. As far as I knew, Roger's father had not been on the scene for years – why suddenly turn up now? It made me feel uneasy.

'Mummy?'

'Mmmm?' I bit absent-mindedly into a biscuit.

'Has Roger's Daddy come to take him home?'

'Oh no,' I said, and then immediately checked myself. 'At least, I doubt it.' It was a horrifying thought. Roger had grown on us, despite being a pain in the neck most of the time. Only last week we had talked again of adopting him one day, if we could, and if he agreed.

'I could go and ask.'

'No.'

'Why not?'

'Helen, just shut up, will you?'

I left the room, and slammed the door. Helen followed me upstairs.

'Sorry, Mummy.' Poor Helen – she had no idea what she could have done. The truth was, she had done nothing – she was simply the nearest target. My heart went out to her.

'No, *I'm* sorry,' I said. 'Let's have a cuddle and forget it. Mummy's just in a bad mood today.'

Joseph Flaherty stayed for a couple of hours, and Roger's broad grin when he had gone made me feel, irrationally, very irritated.

'He's coming next Saturday,' beamed Roger. 'We're going to a match.'

'Match?'

'Football!'

'Thought you didn't *like* football,' I said, sounding even to my own ears like a petulant child.

Roger waved his hands in a dismissive gesture.

'Where's he been, your Dad, all this time?' I asked.

Roger shrugged. 'Here and there. He's been away working, you see. He didn't hear about Mum . . . about me coming into care until a couple of days ago. Says he would never have let them do it.'

My heart sank. 'I see,' I said slowly. 'And . . . where's he living now?'

'Only in Finsbury Park, not far really. He says I can stay the weekend. He's going to take me to my Gran's as well. I like her – we

used to go every Saturday, when we was at me Mum's. She's a bit
loony, but she's all right. My Dad says . . .'

And Roger, for whom 'Dunno' had hitherto been a major
utterance, continued to prattle for a week. He had been discovered
by his own family again. Overnight, Roger had grown roots and an
'I belong' label. And we had begun to lose him.

Roger's sudden joy was hard even though we were genuinely
happy for him. It was hard because whatever we believed about
being objective, at the nerve ends it felt like a rejection of us. It was
ground lost that could never be regained. We were not his natural
family, and Roger, for better or worse, needed his *own* family. It
was cruelly simple.

Roger was very excited about going out for the day with his
Dad; they were to have lunch before the game, and go on
somewhere for tea afterwards. He could hardly concentrate on
anything else – perhaps he was already fantasising about a grand
family reunion.

Saturday dawned bright and clear. For once, Roger did not
have to be coaxed into the bathroom. He was in there a good hour.

'What *is* he doing?' hissed Chris. 'I can smell perfume!'

'It's after-shave,' said Helen knowledgeably.

'After-shave?' we chorused.

Roger was by this time fourteen years old, and not exactly
bewhiskered. 'What's he doing with after-shave?'

'*I* don't know,' said Helen. 'I saw it on his table and asked what it
was. He said it was after-shave, and he has to have it every day.'

'I can hardly wait to see the finished result,' smiled Chris.

Just at that moment we heard the lock on the bathroom door
click, and turned with interest to see what would emerge.

'Well?' said Roger.

I looked him up and down. Ben Sherman shirt, almost clean.
Blue jeans. Yesterday's socks peeping above unpolished black
boots. He looked exactly the same as usual.

'Lovely,' I said. 'Very smart.'

'You don't look any different,' sniffed Helen, before my toe
could reach her ankle.

'Women never notice these things,' said Chris, and winked at
Roger, who smiled knowingly and sauntered down to the living
room, followed by a cloud of *Hai Karate*, to await Joseph
Flaherty's arrival.

He didn't come. No word, no message, just no father. Stubbornly, his face defying sympathy, Roger sat in the living room, all afternoon.

'Come out with us,' said Karen. 'We're going to the flicks. Wayne says there's a great film . . .'

Roger shook his head.

'He's not going to come, Rog,' she said gently. 'You know he's not. Same as my old man, I expect – long on good intentions, short on memory.'

I flinched at the pain in Roger's face and the bitterness in Karen's memory. Roger got up from the sofa.

'I don't care,' he said. Then, catching our expressions, he repeated, 'I don't. There's a good programme on telly, anyway. I didn't really want to miss it.' He stalked off upstairs. Karen raised her eyebrows, sighed, and reached for her coat.

'Tina's asleep – Wayne's just fed her. See you later.'

'Yes, O.K.' I said. I turned my cheek for a kiss automatically, my mind elsewhere.

'Don't worry, Beth – *he'll* be all right!'

'Will *you*?' I suddenly asked. I didn't know why I said it. I felt vulnerable, suddenly aware that the castle we had struggled to build for our hybrid family in the past few months was, after all our efforts, little more than a shack built upon shifting sand.

'I am trying, Beth, really I am. If only Tina weren't so . . . if only . . . oh, I don't know.'

'I'm sorry Karen. I'm just tired. You're doing well, love, all things considered. We're proud of you.'

She hugged me fiercely, sensing I needed it. And then she was gone, with a cheery wave and a slamming of the door. Tina wailed.

Sunday was a black day indeed. Wayne and Karen had rowed the night before, and were not speaking. Neither of them were prepared to talk about it. Wayne had apparently revived his suspicions about Karen and another boy. We gathered this, much later in the afternoon, from Wayne's terse comment that Karen was a 'tart', and Karen's own graphic, 'Up yours, Wayne Cooper!' as she left for the ice rink. She did this against Wayne's express instructions – 'forbidding me like I was a child' – to stay away from there.

Roger sat in the rocking chair in the study, glued to the television set. He watched the morning service, cartoons, the farming programme, the lot. He did join us for lunch, though.

It was a jolly meal. Helen, not wishing to be left out of the general gloom and misery, had complained non-stop all morning about the weather, the boring television, and most of all my meanness in not allowing her to bake while I cooked the Sunday lunch *or* teach her to knit a jumper for her teddy. I was the Worst Mother in the Entire World. Even worse than Becky Jones' Mummy; this, I gathered, was the ultimate humiliation. Helen had no intention of taking time off for lunch, either.

'I don't *like* sweet corn.'

'Don't eat it, then.'

'But then I won't get dessert.'

' 's right.'

'I'll eat half.'

'Fine.'

'I don't like these 'taters, either. Why can't we have chips?'

'Helen, just eat,' said Chris wearily.

'But I don't *like* it.'

I banged down my knife and fork, and took away her plate.

'Right – don't eat it. Go and play.'

'But I want my lunch.'

'No you don't – you just said so.'

Helen started to wail. 'I want my lunch. I want dessert.' This had no effect, so she escalated the protest.

'Gimme my lunch, gimme my lunch, gimme my lunch.' She sounded like a train gathering speed. My hands itched to spank Helen's bottom. But I was young, full of idealism and techniques culled from magazines.

'Calm down, my love,' I said. 'Or you will have to leave the room.'

'Shan't. Want my lunch, want my lunch. Gimme.'

'That's ENOUGH!' I yelled.

In answer, Helen threw her cup on the floor.

Finally, she stormed off upstairs to brood over the injustice of having been born to the Worst Mother in the Entire World – and search for the bright red hand mark. Instinct had overcome, in the end.

Roger, meanwhile, was pushing his food around with a fork, tossing some into his mouth now and then with no enthusiasm. Wayne and Karen ate silently, without tasting the food, avoiding each other's eyes. You could have cut the air between them with a knife. Chris, who had already conducted two services and a Sunday School, had a bad cold. His contribution to the meal was a litany of coughs, sneezes, groans, and the scraping back of a chair as he searched for more handkerchiefs.

The food I had so carefully prepared, because this was the only meal of the week we were all together and I liked it to be a bit special, may as well have been cardboard mock-ups.

'Well, isn't this jolly?' I said grimly.

Wayne smiled weakly. No-one else acknowledged the remark. I made a mental note to stick to ham sandwiches next week. That'ld show them.

Sunday lunch proved to be a typical extract of the whole day. By bedtime I was as gloomy as anyone. It had even started to rain, sunny breezes giving way to great pelting drops beating down on my full clothes line in the garden.

'I'm just going to pretend today never happened,' I told Chris.

'Things'll be better tomorrow, I expect,' he said. With a comforting pat on the head that made me feel like a miserable pet spaniel, Chris rolled over and was instantly asleep.

Chris was right. The next day was better, at least a bit. Roger got a phone call just before he left for school. Obviously his Dad had come up with a satisfactory explanation.

'It was Dad,' he said, as if his expression had not said it all. 'We're going out Thursday night.' He left smiling.

Wayne and Karen were still at loggerheads but a thaw seemed imminent. Karen asked me for a cake recipe for Wayne's birthday in a few days time. And she didn't go to the ice rink. Lately she had been there almost every day. I felt we were pulling out of our bad patch, and decided to capitalise on a faint sense of optimism.

Every year since she was a baby we had taken Helen to Whipsnade Zoo. It was about time to go again.

'Can Roger come? And Tina?'

'If they want to, of course they can,' I said, hoping to get us all together for once. I was not disappointed. We were a complete, if squashed family as we eased into the car and set off. It was a lovely day. The sun shone, and the roads were fairly clear. The animals were unusually sociable. They chased around and played to the gallery for a change, instead of sitting and staring at us from the other side of the compound.

We picknicked in the children's zoo. Helen was attacked by a Jersey calf; a goat almost took Karen up on her offer of Tina as a tasty nibble for tea; a woolly lamb showed a very unsheepish interest in Roger's can of shandy. All in all, it was a wonderful day.

'That was really good,' said Roger on the way home.

'Yeah – we ought to go out together more often,' said Karen.

'What about tomorrow?' suggested Helen hopefully.

Chris and I exchanged satisfied smiles. The day at Whipsnade would be one of our clearest, happiest memories of those few months; not least because our family was on the verge of disintegration.

Wayne and Karen were reunited for Wayne's birthday, and she did indeed bake him a cake. But it was an uneasy reconciliation. Karen spent more and more time at the rink. The programme of taking care of Tina and doing her share of the household chores went to the wall.

'Why don't *you* take Tina to the park?' she would say. 'People only stare at me.' Or, 'Beth – I'll do all this tomorrow, all right?'

The shouting and screaming whenever Tina demanded attention began again. Karen complained of pain: headaches, backaches, sore throats. Every day there seemed to be another problem, another reason why she could not take care of Tina. She still managed to crawl to the ice rink, though.

Chris and I, not knowing what to do, did probably the worst possible thing. We were so worried that Karen was going to lose any sort of bond with Tina, not to mention the flat she had set her heart on, that we pushed too hard. Get her through this, we thought, and when she comes out the other side she'll be stronger, more able to cope.

'Look, Karen. I'm tired too. I don't feel particularly well myself,' I said when she complained. 'And the thing about being a mother is, you just have to keep going. What are you going to do when you have a home of your own and Wayne is at work all day? You won't be able to just give up and hand over to me then, you know. I might be miles away.'

Many times we sat at the old dining room table and talked, hashing and rehashing all the old problems and grievances. Despite all the stresses and strains, despite the spectacular rows which raged and flowed, Karen and I grew very close. Karen used me as a safe habour, where she could vent her rage and frustration.

I understood this and accepted it. What I did not recognise was that I was using Karen too. I was seeking some grand work, the creation of a silk purse from a collection of sows' ears. Then I could prove, to myself as well as others, that we did really know what we were doing – we were 'good' foster parents. I had yet to learn what true success is all about.

Admittedly, things were going very badly. Roger had always been laconic. Now he became positively truculent and went out of his way to be troublesome. He refused to join in any family activity, from a trip to the fair to a general mad clean-up before guests arrived. The television seemed to be on non-stop. Roger was confused and unhappy. We saw it, but could not help him.

Then Wayne and Karen had a fight – a real, punch for punch fight which terrified Helen and showed me how close to defeat we were.

'That's it!' stormed Wayne. 'She can do what she likes. I'm off! I only stuck her for this long because of Tina.' His nose was bleeding slightly.

'Good riddance!' screeched Karen at him as he stalked down the path. Her lip was swollen and there was a red mark on her cheek.

Helen was sobbing. I cuddled her to me, and asked Karen icily what all this was about.

'He keeps going on and on about me not being a proper mother. We've got to do this, do that – he sounds like an old man, the way he goes on. I've had enough.'

'So it would seem,' I said. 'And you're not the only one. Was it really necessary to play out this grand drama in front of the little one?'

Karen at least had the grace to look shamefaced. 'Sorry. But he's just . . . I hate him. I don't ever want to see him again, the pig. That's all.'

'That's *all*?' I shouted, suddenly very angry. 'That's *all*? You've broken up with Tina's father, thrown away her chance of a decent home and a proper family life with a "that's all"? What about Tina, Karen?'

'What about her?' Karen shrugged. 'Let *him* have her. Let him

clean up her mess and stay awake all night and feel ill and tired all the time – *all* the time. I don't care.'

'That's a baby, Karen, not a toy. She's a real live person, and she has only you to count on. You and Wayne are all the family she's got. What are you going to do, split her between you along with the Building Society and the records?'

Karen simply turned on her heel and ran up the stairs, slamming the bathroom door and locking it. Helen's sobs redoubled.

Roger arrived home from school just then. 'What's up?' he said.

'Karen,' was all I could say, being close to tears myself.

'Oh, her again,' and he headed for the staircase. He simply wasn't interested. Roger was no longer ours. Was it because we were giving so much attention to Tina and Karen? Or was it the confusion of loyalties sparked off by contact with his own kith and kin? I just don't know. I suspect it was a combination of the two. Try as I might to recapture the spirit of the day at Whipsnade, Roger simply refused to draw closer.

'Roger, tell us straight. Do you *want* to be a part of this family, or not?' a very exasperated Chris had asked one afternoon.

'Dunno,' he said. Then, 'Well, I got nowhere else, have I? Don't want to go, don't want to stay. Don't care.'

It was deeply wounding, and neither Chris nor I had the experience to be able to draw back from it all and treat it more objectively. We were exhausted, burned out.

Finally, we were discovering that fostering children was not always going to provide the rewards we had grown to expect. There would be no rosy sunset this time.

Helen whined incessantly, confused and clinging. I was worried about the effect of all this upon our innocent daughter, who had probably forgotten what ordinary family life was like. Perhaps she would be permanently marked. I was worried about Karen and Tina being separated, about Karen and Wayne breaking up. I was worried about Roger being let down by his father – or was I more worried that he was perhaps being let down by us, by Chris and me?

I did not know, and was too tired to care much. Round and round the anxiety went, a merry-go-round spinning ever faster. It could not continue, not like this. But I could see no way out, either.

Then a series of events took such decisions out of our hands. A conclusion was at hand – not the one we would have chosen, but an escape back into daylight nonetheless.

I called Neil, to let him know about Wayne and Karen. Karen's feelings for Tina were a real cause for concern. Neil made arrangements to come over to the house.

'I'm sorry, Beth. Looks like she's trying to tell us she just isn't ready to be a Mum.'

'I know,' I said miserably. 'It's awful – we tried so hard, and things went so well for a while there. I wish I knew where we had had gone wrong.'

'Listen, it's no good thinking like that. You've done a great job holding anything together at all for this long. You think Karen would have held on for eight months, in a mother and baby unit? Come on, Beth, be realistic. Success with teenagers is in making contact at all. You've certainly done that with Karen and Roger.'

'Mmm.' Wait until you hear about our record with Roger, I thought.

'Beth, you sound upset. You've done wonders, honestly. You just can't look at it objectively at the moment, that's all. I don't want you and Chris to feel like you've failed, or something.'

Even if we have, I added to the self-pitying silence.

'By the way, Beth, have you had a call from David?'

'No. Should I?' We had not seen Roger's Social Worker for some time.

'He told me he was going to call. The thing is, the Grandmother is making noises about having Roger to live with her.'

'Great,' I said.

'Don't mention it to him, yet,' said Neil. 'It's not final by any means. I just wondered how you'd feel. It'll be hard for you and Chris, if he goes, after you've grown so close. And with all the trouble with Karen as well . . .'

'You'd never call us close if you could see us now,' I said bitterly. 'To be honest, Roger's been a right pain in the neck these last few weeks. He just doesn't want to be here, you know. His real place is with his Dad and his Gran, whatever they do. If he can go to his Gran, it'll be much better for him. Only, if he's going, I think he should go as soon as possible. It will be hard enough.'

'Understood,' said Neil quickly, and said a tactful goodbye.

Another failure to chalk up. Why did we ever decide to be foster parents anyway? We were too young, too inexperienced at life, never mind fostering. We'd taken on far too much, and I could see nothing positive in our contribution at all. I wondered if we had done any of the children we had cared for any good whatsoever. Rock bottom was staring me in the face.

'Come on,' said Chris when I had poured out all my woes. 'Let's go out and buy a freezer.'

'Buy a . . .?' I was absolutely outraged. Hadn't he listened to me at all? 'Chris, our whole life is falling apart – and you want to buy a freezer?'

'Yep. I just worked out this morning we've saved enough. Come on, Beth. You've been going on about how wonderfully life will be organised with a freezer. Proper dinners every night, the old Cordon bleu stacked away for emergencies. Now's your chance to prove it.'

'Chris, stop it! I can't think about blasted freezers.'

Chris held up his hand for silence and opened the window.

'Helen, get your mother's coat. We're going to buy a freezer.'

'Whoopee!'

I followed them out to the car in silence. As we wandered round the store, however, I realised how well Chris knew me. Of course I couldn't forget all the problems besetting us, any more than he could. But just being out of the house, just the three of us, doing something very ordinary and undramatic, was a tonic. For once, we were a regular, unremarkable family, making an ordinary family purchase. And I had wanted a freezer for a long time, it was true.

Chris, with the determined air of one setting out to meet a mighty challenge, noted down all the sizes, prices, offers and measurements. We adjourned to a coffee bar to ponder our final decision. By this time, I felt almost cheerful. Chris scribbled diagrams of the kitchen and dining room, the latter being a more likely site, and made a quick table to assess the best deal.

'What are you doing, Daddy?'

'Sssh.'

'Mummy, what is Daddy doing?'

'He's making lists of all the freezers, Helen.'

'Why does he have to make lists?'

'You will find out when you're bigger, Helen, that Daddy has to make lists about *everything*.' I raised my voice slightly. 'It's called a compulsion, dear – poor Daddy can't help it.'

A few curious glances came our way.

'It's called method, Helen. Take no notice of your mother. I am working out which freezer is the very best one for us. Your mother, you see, would just go in and choose the prettiest-looking one, if she were by herself.'

'So would I.' Helen snuggled up to me and looked at her father as if he were a rather embarrassing elderly relative. Then, taking pity on him, she leaned across the table and said encouragingly, 'It looks very nice, Daddy. When we get home I'll lend you my crayons and you can colour it in, if you like.'

'That was nice,' I said as we drove up to the house, with the freezer duly ordered and paid for. I leaned over to give Chris a kiss.

'Whoo – I saw you!' came a delighted whoop from the back seat. Helen was fast approaching *that* age.

'We must do this kind of thing more often,' smiled Chris. 'After all, you can never have enough freezers about the place.'

These pathetic jokes continued up the path, through the door and into the hallway. We were still laughing like a couple of emptying drains when we fell into the living room – and encountered a strange man sitting on our sofa. He was tall and middle-aged, and he stood up nervously when he saw us.

'Er – hallo,' said Chris. 'Who are you?'

'Ted Holroyd,' the man answered. The name meant nothing. 'My wife's upstairs with Karen.'

Clearly this was meant to explain all. When he saw our blank incomprehension, he tried again. 'We've come for the baby.'

'What baby?' Chris asked, but I had jumped on a couple of steps mentally, and headed for the stairs.

Sure enough, Karen was in her room, busily packing a suitcase. Tina's clothes and toys were everywhere; all the cupboards and drawers had been turned out. Both Karen and Mrs Holroyd jumped when I entered.

'Karen, what *are* you doing?'

Karen straightened up. 'I've found someone who wants to adopt Tina. They're going to take her today.'

8

Farewell and Failure

At first I thought Karen must be playing some sort of joke, or had temporarily taken leave of her senses. It was difficult to believe, either, that the Holroyds thought they could just collect a baby as if she were a three-piece-suite, nearly new, reasonable offers. But they were certainly going to give it their best try, and expressed innocent surprise that I should feel they were doing wrong.

'She's not in care, is she?' said Karen. 'She's *my* baby; it's up to me to decide her future.'

'Don't be naïve, Karen. Behaviour like this is the surest way to prove you're not fit to be her mother and have her *taken* from you. Are you honestly telling me you can see nothing wrong in it?'

'Yes.'

'Then why', I asked slowly, 'did you wait until Chris and I were out?'

Karen could not answer that. I looked at Mrs Holroyd. Explanation from her, as a reasonable and supposedly responsible adult, was more than necessary. She looked uncomfortable, but said nothing.

'Mrs Holroyd?' I felt like a schoolteacher reasoning with a wayward pupil. This was ridiculous – the woman was almost twice my age. 'Surely you can see that this isn't going to work. It's hardly the action of a responsible parent, is it? No agency on earth will allow you to adopt a child, if you do this now.'

'No,' she agreed simply. 'What shall we do?'

'I'll call Social Services,' I said. 'We'll get this sorted now.'

I was amazed to hear the calm, even tone of my voice. Inside I was shaking like a leaf, and had not the faintest idea what to do next. It's very unusual to be able to locate the social worker you need in times of crisis, and I only hoped, as I dialled the area office, that the duty worker would believe my story and not regard it as a hoax. For once, though, Neil was in. I explained the situation.

'What?' He said disbelievingly. '*What?*'

'It's true,' I insisted, tension giving way to a giggle. 'Seems Karen's gone into the mail-order baby business. Oh Neil, you'd better come round, if you can.'

'I'm on my way right now,' he answered. 'They must be idiots, these people, to think they can do this.'

It was a very uncomfortable half-hour while we waited for Neil. I handed round tea and tried to make polite conversation, but soon gave up. The situation was not helped by the irrepressible Helen who, despite warning looks from Chris and I, would keep asking questions: 'What's going on? Is Tina going away? Is that lady going to be Tina's Mummy?'

'Helen, we don't know what's going to happen at the moment. Now stop asking questions,' I said, finally having mercy on poor Mrs Holroyd. Then Roger poked his head round the door.

'I'm back. What's going on?'

Helen took him by the hand and left the room, telling him in a stage whisper that Karen had sold Tina to these people and now Mummy was telling her to give the money back. Mrs Holroyd went even whiter and her husband took her hand. Still angry and confused, I was nonetheless a bit sorry for this gentle-looking couple. I wondered what Karen had told them.

Once Neil arrived, Chris and I decided we did not want to be involved and waited in the kitchen, huddled together in miserable silence. Roger and Helen poked their heads in.

'They're snogging – leave 'em,' I heard Roger say.

'What's snogging?' As they went up the stairs again, I heard the beginning of Roger's very graphic definition. He made it sound quite off-putting.

There was the sound of raised voices next door; Karen's almost hysterical shouting, Neil's deeper tones. My heart sank. A couple of minutes later the front door slammed. We went out into the hallway.

The living room door was open. Karen and Neil sat together on the sofa. Tina slept peacefully in her pram. The Holroyds had gone.

'Well?' asked Chris.

'Karen just doesn't feel able to cope with Tina. The Holroyds, it turns out, are not complete strangers – they're friends of Wayne's family. What we've worked out is that Tina will stay here with you, if you're agreeable, while the Holroyds go through the approval process for fostering and adoption. We'll do all that as fast as we can – she should be able to move in two or three weeks.'

I nodded dumbly. 'And you, Karen?'

Karen was not able to speak, and just shook her head. Her eyes were red; she looked very young and pale.

'Karen does not want anything more to do with Tina. She doesn't want the flat we've found either,' explained Neil.

I could not comprehend or believe this, but it was not going to be any use arguing with Karen in her present state. For the first time it began to dawn on me that she might be really depressed – we had been too close, the change too gradual, to see it before. But this was not the same girl as our laughing teenage Mum of three months ago.

'So we look after Tina,' I said. 'Fine. And you can just hold her and look after her whenever you want to, with no pressure . . .'

'No!' Karen sprang to her feet. 'I can't stay in the same house as her, Beth. I've got to get away. I'm sorry . . .' she started sobbing again, and I put my arms around her.

'Oh my love, you have nothing to be sorry about. You tried. You tried, Karen: lots of kids wouldn't even have done that.'

It would have helped me to be angry with her, but I could not avoid feeling it was our failure more than hers. We had made so many mistakes that were way past redemption now. We were about to lose Karen, Tina and probably Roger too, in one fell blow. Life with them may have become intolerable, but losing them like this would crush us. Chris and I could never be the same again.

All this was running through my mind even as I hugged Karen and listened to Neil's arrangements. He would collect Karen after the weekend, when hostel accommodation had been arranged.

'I have to go,' said Neil finally. 'I wish I could stay a bit longer and talk things through, but . . .' he took out his diary. 'Look, let's get together towards the end of next week. Say, Friday afternoon?'

He would be coming to pick up the pieces, I thought.

'Good,' said Chris, and showed him out.

Karen was finally calm.

'Well,' I attempted a smile. 'You'd better start packing, I suppose.' For the first time, I could not even come close to understanding Karen, or guess what she was thinking. This girl was a stranger. 'Will you let us know how you get on, Karen?'

'Of course. I . . . hope I can still come and see you. You've been like parents to me, you and Chris. You know that.' She kissed me lightly on the cheek and went to the door. 'I'll miss you,' she said, and left.

'Then why go?' I wanted to say. 'Why can't we make it work? Why?'

The next day, before we even had time to mentally pick ourselves up off the floor, Roger's social worker informed us that the Grandmother was going to take charge of Roger. All being well, he would move in at the end of the month – that gave us about three weeks.

'That soon?' I whispered.

'You did say you wanted him to move as soon as possible. When I spoke to Chris, he said you had a holiday coming up. We thought it best to have all the loose ends tied up before then.'

Our holiday; I had forgotten all about it, but we had indeed booked a cottage in Cornwall. We had booked it a long time ago, when it was taken for granted Roger would be coming too. I remembered him moaning about how boring it would be, and how I had known he would make everybody miserable. Yes, it made sense for him to go before we left. Chris and Helen and I needed that holiday.

'Do you want us to tell Roger, David? I think his Grandmother has been hinting to him already.'

'Yes, I think you're right. But I'll tell him when he comes to the office. You know he's dropping in after school tonight?'

'He didn't tell us. But then, he tells us very little these days.'

'I'm sorry it's all been so awful these past few weeks, Beth. You and Chris have really been through the mire, haven't you?' said David. His voice was warm and sympathetic, and made me want to cry.

'It's not just his fault, you know. We've had so much trouble with Karen, Roger and Helen were sort of pushed to the back of the queue. Taking Karen on was the worst thing we could have done from Roger's point of view. At least a place with his Gran is what he really wanted. I hope it works out for him.'

And that was that. Roger arrived home for dinner not looking exactly overjoyed, but not willing to talk either. He received the news about Karen with mild surprise but no comment. Of his own imminent removal, he would only say: 'I don't really want to leave here, but I don't really want to stay either. I don't care either way.' This smoke screen gave us no clue about his hopes for the future.

The next three weeks dragged on and on; it felt like a very extended tooth extraction. On the eve of Karen's departure we had a special farewell dinner. If you can imagine eating Christmas lunch with a bereaved family right before the funeral, you will just about catch the mood of the party.

The following week Tina was taken to the Holroyds. I knew I would miss her. In a way, though, I was relieved to have time to myself again. At least Tina's future looked bright, with two loving mature parents who could give her a real home. The Holroyds were going to foster Tina with a view to adopting her when it was possible.

And the week after that, Roger left. We packed his possessions into cardboard boxes, and Chris loaded them into the car. Then we stood around wondering what to say. Chris was going to drive Roger to his grandmother's house. Helen and I were staying behind. Great tears rolled down Helen's little cheeks: I had cried enough, and just felt hard and numb.

'It'll be quiet,' said Roger.

'Yes. Yes, it will.'

'Goodbye, then.'

'Goodbye.' I gave him a quick, embarrassed peck on the cheek. For once, he didn't squirm. 'Be happy – come see us, sometime, eh? You'll always be welcome.'

'Yeah. 'Bye, Helen.' He bent down and Helen's arms tightened around his neck.

'See us soon,' she said.

'Yeah, 'Bye, then.'

We watched them drive off and stood at the gate until they were out of sight. Helen was sobbing openly – I took her hand.

'Come on, Helen. We'll be all right, you know. We'll be sad for a while and then we'll be all right. And you know what? Daddy and I will have lots more time to play with you now – that'll be great.

Let's find something good to do right now, to cheer ourselves up.'

Helen wiped her face on her sleeve. 'Jam tarts?'

'Why not?' I said. 'Loads and loads of jam tarts. 'Cos the freezer will be here tomorrow.'

'Can I make *all* the pastry?' Children are so fickle.

'Of course you can.' I followed her down the front path and shut the door.

Our house was silent and empty. So much for fostering. No-one was likely to ask us again in a hurry. And indeed, I did not ever want the privilege of being someone's foster mother ever again.

9

Starting Over

Chris and I arrived at our holiday destination exhausted, emotional and physical wrecks after weeks of worry and sleepless nights. I had expected to feel very unhappy, but a great strain had been lifted from our shoulders. The relief that it was all over far outweighed the sense of dejection and failure that had initially threatened to overpower us.

We slept late in the mornings, knowing Helen was quite safe in the enclosed garden, prancing around in her pyjamas with a handful of biscuits. The cottage stood on a small mixed farm. Often the farmer's wife came by to collect Helen to play with her own two children. Or she would take her to see the latest newborns. Ducks, geese, puppies, chickens and even a foal were all born during our stay, and Helen was absolutely entranced by it all.

It was late Spring, and the air was cool and clear. Hope and beauty blossomed everywhere; it was difficult not to be soothed and lifted. We tramped around the countryside, visited cattle markets and stately homes, drank gallons of lemonade and scrumpy. We played cards and Scrabble far into the night, forbidding each other newspapers or television.

Helen had a wonderful time. She was fascinated, embarrassingly enough, by lavatories. 'Helen's loo period,' Chris dubbed it. Every single loo we passed had to be visited, and judgement passed.

'That's a good one,' she would say as she rejoined us. 'Wooden seats!' Or 'Hmm – no loo paper and floor's wet. Not as good as . . .' Or just a graphic, 'Yukk!'

By far the most entertaining was the one at the trade fair in Cornwall. It consisted of a plank suspended over a ditch, with minimum privacy. I, coward, was cross-legged all the way home, but Helen spent a good part of the afternoon there. 'But I'm *bursting*,' she would insist when I told her three times in an hour was enough for anyone's bladder.

We stayed a full fortnight and returned to London feeling like different people. The house no longer felt so empty. It was nice to have a chance to catch up on some reading, take Helen to the park more often, do a bit of decorating. And then there was the new 'baby', the freezer. I named her Patricia, for no good reason. She had an appetite quite as voracious as any child.

I spent a full week baking and cooking and stewing – and standing guard over the food until it was safely stowed in the freezer.

Chris, being a glutton despite his sickeningly skinny frame, has always claimed he is kept on a starvation diet. He could not see the logic of making beef bourgignon and lemon sorbet for the freezer and feeding *him* hamburgers and ice cream.

'We want to have something good on standby, in case we have guests unexpectedly for dinner,' I told him, straight out of my new Owner's Guide.

'We're having guests *tonight*,' he insisted.

'Who?'

'Well, I don't exactly know yet, but if it's the only way to get a decent meal, I'll find someone.'

In the end we compromised – Chris and Helen were allowed to try everything before I froze the remainder. But requests for second helpings were treated with the scorn they deserved.

At first, we decided not to take any more foster children at all. Neil, however, had been quite insistent that this was, in his words, 'plain daft'.

'Neil, whatever you say, our handling of Karen and Roger was not exactly brilliant, was it?' I said.

'Look, you did more than many would have done. And you gave Karen the chance to find out if she could cope. You helped her face up to not being able to, as well. And Roger was a different kid after a couple of months with you – you know he was. If the pull to his own family made him react badly, that could hardly be called your fault, could it?'

'We sound quite splendid,' I told him, not believing a word.

'You made mistakes – so did I. But I still consider it all to have been a good, worthwhile experience – for the kids, as well as you.

I'd place a child with you again, any time. So come on, what do you say?'

'You know,' said Chris slowly, 'I think the real problem was we took on too much, too soon. And perhaps we made a mistake taking teenagers at all, while Helen is so young . . .'

'I don't agree,' Neil cut in, 'But I can see it'll take a while to get over the last experience. Why not take a few months break, before you decide finally whether you want to carry on or not?'

'I don't want to give up,' said Chris. 'But it's Beth who has the most to do with the children.'

They both looked at me, waiting for judgement.

'Little ones,' I said. 'Let's go back to young children. I can handle that, I think.'

I was not a great lover of babies, but at least they are straighforward creatures. You feed one end, mop up the other, wear washable clothes and revise your stock of nursery rhymes. Yes, I could do that. With Helen at school all day, I missed sticky little hands and Goldilocks and her three bears.

There followed a short succession of toddlers, who brought sunshine into our home and boosted our flagging confidence. The first of these was Paddy, the eighteen-month-old son of a local street trader. Apparently his father had been involved in some deal which had gone wrong. The other traders were after him and he had upped and gone 'on the run' as Paddy's mother put it. She was a slender, attractively painted woman for whom the birth of Paddy, seven years after his sister, had been an unexpected nuisance. This was never said aloud, but became clear as time went on. Once Paddy came to us, she never visited him at all. The older children dropped by quite often, always with a hazy excuse why Mum couldn't make it today. 'She might be able to come tomorrow.'

Paddy did not seem too bothered. He was remarkably quiet for a toddler, not given to tantrums at all. His sister and brothers gave him a lot of affection, for which I was very glad. Paddy was especially in need of physical contact. My heart went out to him as he followed me around the house, crying whenever I went out of sight, beaming when I came back into view. At night he slept well, in a cot in Helen's room. In the morning he would climb out and tug at our bedclothes.

Usually I could sympathise with our foster children's own

parents, but Paddy's mother had me beaten. Persistently I telephoned, every couple of days, to let her know he was all right, and what he had been doing. She was simply not interested. She would listen politely, and then tell me what a whining, difficult little bugger he was at home.

'Mick's the only one who could ever handle the little so-and-so,' she said. 'And Gawd knows where *he* is.'

We found out where Mick was after Paddy had been with us three weeks. He was up North somewhere – and furious. Apparently his wife had forgotten to tell him that she had put Paddy into care, although they had been in touch by phone. He found out, as they say, from a mutual friend.

Paddy was removed and returned home within twenty-four hours. We tried not to think about his mother too much, comforting ourselves with the knowledge that he had other members of the family to count on.

Within two days of Paddy's departure, Charlie arrived. This was a two-week stay while his mother, a single parent, was in hospital. Charlie was only ten months old, but he was a big lad, weighing almost thirty pounds. He was delightful, full of smiles and very accommodating. Charlie submitted to all Helen's patting and preening and attempts at nappy changing without a murmur.

Helen was in her element with babies. She would wipe bottoms, kiss hairless heads 'to make it all grow', and share treasured toys – at least for a while. At the first sign of what Helen regarded as inappropriate treatment of one of her possessions, it would be unceremoniously reclaimed.

This 'littlies' period was just what we needed. The placements were all short and fairly straightforward. They also provided, through our contact with the families of the babies, a detailed and varied education in that mysterious and evasive topic, Life.

Charlie's appetite was voracious. He was not exactly a picky eater. Every day he made a thorough search of the house, crawling from one room to another with a great sense of purpose. He would haul himself upright by a chair or coffee table, and mark out his targets in his mind's eye. Cups, glasses, and teapots provided delicious dregs to swig and wipe the floor with. Sometimes there was a forgotten sweet or a bone hidden by the cat. It is due to Charlie that I know cigarette ends are totally indigestible. He was particularly partial to a filled ashtray, and I had to be very careful

to clear away properly when we had guests for dinner. If I left the work until the morning, I could count on Charlie being way ahead of me.

Another of our short run of little folk at this time was to be the one who stood out in my memory, although it was only a 'one night stand'.

This one began, as always, with a telephone call. It was five o'clock – panic hour for social workers with unresolved cases on their hands – so I was not at all surprised to hear Chris say, 'For you. Social Worker.'

Much to the annoyance of Chris, social workers wanting to place children would never speak to *him*; if he answered the telephone they would always ask if *Mrs* Miller was at home.

The fact was, I relied on Chris quite heavily, especially for entertaining the smaller children and feeding any baby that we might have with us, while I prepared the dinner. Just as I was reaching breaking point, kicking toys across the floor and screaming for quiet:

'Turn that radio down . . . look, you can't possibly want to go *again*. I don't *know* where it is, now for pete's sake LEAVE ME ALONE!' I would hear the key turning in the lock and feel a flood of relief as I fell in love with my husband all over again simply for arriving at just the right moment.

'Hallo – they're all yours,' would be my greeting, as I bolted into the kitchen and slid the door firmly shut.

Our kitchen was too tiny to have a conventional door, although the house was a large Victorian one. It was more of a ship's galley. Once inside, I could reach cupboards, cooker and sink without taking a step. Anything that required space for rolling, chopping etc. had to be done in the dining room. This was hell when we had a dinner party, but great when I needed to get away. The door was too heavy for the children to slide open, so they could not get at me!

Chris, whose work meant that he often spent the day totally alone in his office, would greet the children with great gusto. As I reached the depths at the end of the day, his batteries would be fully charged, so we at least made a good team. For Chris, the noise and confusion, and the clamours for attention, were just what he needed after a silently contemplative day. With one cry of 'Put the kettle on,' he would be out in the garden playing football, or changing a baby's nappy while listening to the jumbled accounts of the day's events.

Meanwhile I sat on a stool in my tiny fortress, glassy-eyed and smelling of sherry. I hummed and stirred and clattered the odd saucepan lid whenever there was a childish rap on the door: 'I'm busy cooking dinner – go and ask daddy!'

All this seemed to be ignored by the Social Services Department. We never managed to work out why Chris got second class rating as a foster parent. Several times we had half-jokingly pleaded for 'equal rights for foster fathers'. Nonetheless, whether it was something to do with the way information was recorded on the central files, or just plain stereotype thinking, all maintenance cheques and phone calls came to me.

This particular call was about fifteen-month-old Jody, whose mother was on the brink of a nervous breakdown. The plan was to place Jody with us just for a few days while the situation was sorted out – it was an emergency placement which needed to start immediately.

After a brief consultation with Chris, I agreed quite happily. July and August were the quietest months for Chris. With no major festivals and most of his parishioners away on holiday he was also able to spend more time at home, and we had a holiday coming up which would give us time to rest and recover from what had been a very busy few months.

'They'll be with us in an hour or so,' I told Chris. 'I'll go and set up the travel cot in our room – it will feel more secure there. By the way, is Jody a boy or a girl – isn't it one of those bi-sexual names?'

Chris frowned. 'It had better be a boy. Charlie and I don't want to be outnumbered, do we?' he grinned at Charlie, who was busy making patterns on the floor.

Making patterns on the floor? All through the telephone call I'd watched him, and yet somehow not seen what he was doing. Only now did it sink in. Charlie had somehow got into the kitchen cupboard and found an open packet of tea, which he had promptly upended on the polished pine floor of the dining room before swirling his fingers in it. Chris and Helen were happily watching him, assuming that since I had not commented, it must be one of my 'creative play' ideas. A little weird, but then so were most of my ideas. I did not like to admit that I had stared at him without registering a thing. Anyway, the damage was done now; there was tea everywhere and the whole floor would have to be swept. There seemed no harm in doing it half-an-hour later and letting Charlie make the most of it. I tried telling him how naughty he was but that crooked grin (Charlie's teeth were already a dentist's nightmare) melted my heart.

'You'd smack *me* if I did that,' protested Helen, with a seven year old's sense of injustice.

'He's a baby, and doesn't know any better. Go on, you may as well help him with the art work.'

Soon the pair of them were engrossed in the simple and time-honoured pleasure of making a mess for someone else to clear up. Chris and I sat down for an unexpectedly peaceful pot of tea.

Jody turned out to be a girl, a very beautiful white haired little angel with watchful blue eyes. Her mother, Jackie, came in with her. She was severely depressed and clearly not really in touch with the real situation. She said very little as the social worker explained that they were on their way to the hospital, where they expected Jackie would be kept in. Although Jody had a father who lived with them, Jackie did not want him to have the care of Jody. They were not married, so the legal rights over the child were all hers. It seemed that she was worried he might use her illness to take Jody away from her. So, he would only be able to visit, to make sure Jody had settled with us.

Jody herself was silently watchful while all this was going on, and made no noise as her mother took off her own bracelet, a bangle with stars engraved on it, and pressed it into Jody's little hands in some sort of symbolic gesture. Then they left, and I watched Jody anxiously, expecting an outburst. But still she made no sound.

Family dinner was quite an astonishing affair for Jody, used to being the only child at the table. Chris and Helen, who both relished arguments, particularly totally pointless ones, lost no time in sinking their teeth into each other. Where they found new material for this regular meal-time repartee was a mystery to me. This time it was all about whether a hippo could open its mouth wider than a crocodile or not. Chris had studied biology among his Science 'A' levels, and Helen was fresh back from a school trip to the zoo ('where we did *hundreds* of worksheets on *all* the animals'), so both were experts in this field and confident of their claims.

Charlie, who found everything life had to offer amusing, chuckled with glee at both of them as they waved first forks and then dessert spoons in animated discussion. He thought they were playing a game, and joined in enthusiastically, dropping milk jelly in blobs all over the table and Jody's high chair.

Jody watched, round-eyed. A slight, shy smile creased the corners of her mouth once or twice when Chris or I helped her with her food. But she shrank away when Charlie offered her a share in his rusk, and could not be persuaded to join in the bedtime sing-song and tickle-fight. She had not uttered a sound since her arrival, only shaking her head in response to our attentions.

But that night, as I tucked her into the old cot and smoothed her hair, she started to cry softly. Picking her up, I held her in my arms as I knelt on the bedroom floor. She nuzzled into my neck, clinging tightly, so tightly, as though afraid to let go.

There is nothing that tears at the heart more painfully than the sound of a grieving baby. In moments of hurt, bewilderment and loss only a mother – your *own* mother – will do. Only she can soothe the hurt and chase away the shadows. And Jody was lost, bewildered and frightened. She could not even begin to understand what was happening. An abandoned child in an unfamiliar house, Jody had only a stranger's body to cling to. I did not feel or smell the same, I knew that, yet she clung to me, because there was no-one else. I shed a silent tear with her. And I knew again why we fostered: it was because even a caring stranger is better than no-one at all.

10

Stella

Stella was an unexpected Christmas present, a sort of orphan from the storm. Had we known what was coming, we would probably never have taken her in. And yet, when we look back over the years, we remember her with increasing fondness and laughter.

It was December 22nd and the Miller household was operating in overdrive. Chris was rarely to be seen, except at mealtimes. Then he would eat in an absent-minded daze, his mind on higher things. There would be a sporadic muttering over the marmalade at breakfast, punctuated by an occasional wail, such as:

'Six extra services – six!' or, 'Did we sing "While Shepherds Watched" on Christmas Eve last year?'

This particular Christmas was going to be a very unusual one, I reflected as I poured a second cup of coffee. Through the window I watched snowflakes drifting lazily across the wintry garden, complete with snowman. Firstly, it was almost sure to be a real 'white' Christmas. Secondly, I had just about completed my Christmas preparations, an unheard-of achievement. The presents lay wrapped under the shimmering, fresh-scented tree and the freezer was full of home-baked Christmas goodies. For once in my life, I would not be spending Christmas Eve and the early hours of Christmas morning madly finishing off presents and peeling vegetables. Our house was strangely peaceful, and felt almost empty. Just Chris, Helen and I sat at the table that day, looking forward to a quiet, family Christmas.

When the call came it was Mary Reinhard herself – Chief Fostering and Adoption Officer for the borough. She had the tact and diplomacy of a bulldozer and her name was spoken with trepidation in many departments of the town hall, but I had a grudging admiration for her. Mary was a human powerpack who pleaded, coaxed and bullied her way through all adversity to get what she wanted. Mary Reinhard was rarely defeated.

The situation, it seemed, was desperate – a seventeen-year-old girl with literally nowhere to go. A supervised flat was being made ready but would not be finished for another two weeks. Could we help?

'Where is she now?' I asked.

'Oh. Well, at the moment she is in a secure unit in Croydon.' Mary hurried on before this information could sink in – secure units were little more than juvenile lock-ups, I had heard, where those youngsters who were out of control were put. 'But officially they should release her tomorrow. They tell me she is a reformed character and they're really pleased with her. She is very keen to be out of the unit for Christmas.'

I pictured in my mind bleak empty rooms and grim faced staff. Then I looked around me at the shiny red and gold decorations on the tree, the sparkling angels and the Christmas candles on the table. We always entered into the material celebrations of Christmas with great gusto, but we never forgot what it was really all about. Every year, I was warmed by the beauty of our home at Christmas, by the story of the Christ-child who held a central place amidst all the worldly glitter. Who could turn away a child at such a time?

Suffused by a warm glow which was partly the time of year and partly the two large sherries before lunch, I said expansively, 'Oh yes, no problem. I'm in all-day tomorrow – bring her round in the afternoon sometime.'

So it was arranged. I invaded the heavy silence of Chris's study to tell him the news. Chris stared at me open-mouthed.

'Beth, only this morning you were saying how lovely it was to have some peace at least!'

'I know.'

'So – why?'

'I don't know.' I really didn't. 'I should have talked it over with you first – do you mind?'

Chris sat back in his chair and smiled one of his most delicious smiles, a slow teasing grin which reached right up to his eyes, bright blue in the afternoon light.

'You always were a sucker for a hard luck story,' he said.

'*Do* you mind?' I persisted.

'No, of course not.'

Helen, who had slipped into the room and busied herself as usual with the biscuit barrel Chris kept by his desk, was listening intently to the conversation.

'Is Stella coming to stay?'

'Yes, just for a couple of weeks.'

'Is she a big girl?'

'Yes, seventeen. Like . . .' I searched for someone to compare her with, since seventeen meant little to Helen, who was only just seven. 'Like Uncle Jim.'

She chortled. 'No, not like *him*.'

'Yes. Seventeen. They're the same,' I insisted.

Helen's laugh was like a drain emptying. She was almost doubled at the joke. Chris and I looked at each other, mystified.

'Uncle Jim's a *boy*, Mummy. So they're not the same, unless . . .' she could hardly get the words out, 'unless she's got hairs on her tummy.' Chris and I exchanged the pained looks of a parent whose child is at the 'knock knock' stage. The day a child discovers humour marks a watershed in its parents' career. The joke phase is surely the most boring period of a child's development ever to be lived through. When you have forced yourself to laugh at the same joke fifty-nine times you take it in your stride and pump out laughs with the automatic regularity of an over-generous fruit machine. Helen, though, was satisfied; she had scored again, and this latest witticism was good for another fifty-eight repeats yet.

'Anyway,' I stood up and took the third biscuit from Helen's hand, replacing it in the barrel – 'she'll be here tomorrow afternoon, around three.'

'Fine. You know I'll be too busy to do much for the next few days but you have my unstinting support from the sidelines. Now, stop cluttering up my study and go and do something useful – I'll have a cup of tea in half-an-hour or so.'

He turned ungraciously to his typewriter. Our audience was over. I bowed and scraped my way backwards to the door, touching an imaginery forelock. Chris merely waved an imperious hand, responding to my sarcasm with, 'Be gone, wench.'

Helen was making a last-ditch attempt at the biscuits. I pulled her away.

'Stella's just like Jesus,' she suddenly announced.

'Jesus?' I queried.

'We're in for some of her mother's logic, I expect,' said Chris wearily.

'Jesus had nowhere to go, either.'

'Come on then, let's go and put some clean sheets on the manger.' I led her away.

It was our tradition at Christmas to hang up red felt stockings with our names on them. We had a spare one, so it was just a question of cutting Stella's name out of a piece of cloth and gluing it in place. The stockings were hung on the living room wall until Christmas Eve.

It was the first Christmas we had shared in our home with anyone, and as I cut the 'S' for Stella, and remembered Christmases past, I wondered what Stella would make of us, of our Christmas. And I wondered what to put in her stocking; we had no idea even of what she looked like, still less what her interests were, and I had forgotten to ask Mary Reinhard. Time was short, so I decided to look around the local department store and see what I could get. Without any idea of size or colouring I was limited. I pictured the sixteen year old I had taught in my C.S.E. English classes in my brief career as a teacher, and hoped for the best.

Stella was not like any of the girls in my English class. Her face was fine-boned, the features attractively delicate – at least, what I could see of them. Exactly half of Stella's face was covered by a carefully styled curtain of jet black hair. The one hazel eye which was visible glowed with vitality under its burden of black mascara, the only make-up Stella wore. Her skin seemed to be deathly white against the unnatural blackness of the hair, but she looked healthy enough. Drainpipe jeans and a very baggy T-shirt under – was it a man's donkey jacket? – completed the look.

I groaned inwardly as I recalled the eyeshadow kit, the tights, the romantic novel and the cute cuddly rabbit clutching scented bath oil, which even now waited in their shiny wrappings to be packed into Stella's stocking. They were hardly appropriate gifts for *this* young lady.

Once the introductions had been made and the social worker had left, Stella came to find me in the kitchen, where I was washing up. Automatically she took the tea towel and started to dry the cups and saucers – the first foster child ever to help out without being asked.

'Thanks,' I smiled at her, trying to conceal my surprise.

'Oh, that's O.K. Listen, I'm really grateful to you for having me – didn't know what I was going to do. So thanks a lot.'

This was getting better and better – a charmer with manners!

I nodded at the tea towel in her hands. 'I hope it will be a pleasure,' I said and we laughed together.

I had assumed Stella would be staying in over Christmas, having lived out of the swing of things for some time, but it was soon apparent Stella had lots of friends. She made two calls soon after arriving, to put her return to town on the grapevine. The phone did not seem to stop ringing for the rest of the evening.

'Hallo, is Stella there?'

'Can I speak to Stella, please?'

'Stella? Oh, sorry – is she there?'

Soon she had organised a shopping trip and a party for Christmas Eve, Christmas Day at the children's home she had once lived in, and Boxing Day with her elder brother at his flat in Palmers Green. It seemed we were to have our quiet Christmas after all; clearly, Stella saw us simply as providers of food and shelter. We did not know whether to be relieved or sorry. We *had* looked forward to Christmas on our own, but there was a definite charm and *joie de vivre* about Stella that made her irresistibly good to be with – vitality oozed from every pore. Helen was entranced, and stared at Stella at every opportunity, trying to catch a glimpse of the hidden eye. I even caught her peeping through the keyhole when Stella was in the bathroom preparing for the first of her series of parties. She was in the bathroom for nearly two hours, and left the house looking exactly the same as when she arrived, though presumably a good deal cleaner. (At least the cuddly rabbit's bath oil appeared to have been the right choice.)

When Chris, on one of his rare appearances, told her not to forget to write down where she would be, Stella was undisguisedly amused.

'That's really sweet!' she exclaimed. 'Just like you'd imagine an indulgent Daddy to be.' She wrote down all the details with elaborate care. I had a sneaky feeling that if we were to phone the number she gave us later there would be no-one there, but I squashed this ignoble suspicion and waved her off cheerily, having lent her a door key. 'Don't wait up.' Stella arrived home just before 4 a.m., waking me even though she was clearly trying to be quiet.

Inexperienced at our stairs, she creaked her way to the bathroom and was apparently sick. The sound of running water and the cloths being wrung out told me she was at least sober enough to clear up after herself. I rolled over and went back to sleep.

The next day was Christmas Eve and there was frenzied activity, with Chris desperately trying to type the service folder and finish his sermon for Christmas Day, as well as finding replacement readers for the Watchnight service in the face of a local 'flu epidemic. Meanwhile I did some hasty last-minute alterations to costumes before ironing them for the Sunday School's Christmas play, and prepared the rustling paper twists containing an apple and some sweets for each child at the service. Into this hullaballoo Stella appeared about lunchtime, with a sheepish grin.

'Sorry. Overslept. Too much to drink.'

'So I heard.'

'Ah. Sorry, Beth. Still, you're only young once, as my old granny would have said if I'd ever had one.' She tweaked Helen's nose and produced a toffee with a true magician's flourish.

'Um, Beth, can you give me some money? I've only got a pound and I need to do some shopping yet.'

Ann, who was Stella's social worker, had assured me over the telephone that Stella would have plenty of money, since she was going to give her the usual Christmas allowance as well as a clothing grant before she came. So Stella's request, though reasonable enough, surprised me.

'Didn't Ann give you any money?' I asked.

'No. Why, should she? I thought you got the maintenance cheque from Social Services and then you gave me pocket money. Isn't that how it works?'

'Yes, usually. But Ann said . . . oh look, never mind, she must have forgotten. It's just that I can't get to a bank now.'

'I'm afraid we don't accept credit cards, Madam,' said Stella solemnly, and winked at Helen. I surveyed the contents of my purse, which was always bulging but rarely with money.

'Here, I can let you have eight pounds.' I handed the notes over. 'When we see Ann, we must sort this out – she says you're owed Christmas money and some clothing grant from before you came.'

'Oh good,' said Stella vaguely. 'Well, I'm going to hit the town tonight. May I have a key? I'll probably be very late.'

'Listen, Stella.' I hesitated. Usually we stipulated such things as coming-in times right from the start. However, there really seemed to be little point in laying down the law with someone who was a very temporary visitor. Finally I just said, 'Don't be as late as last night – we worry about you.'

'Yes, O.K. See you – Happy Christmas!' And she was gone.

Christmas Eve was everything I had hoped it would be, that year. Snow glistened on the lamp-lit pavements and snuggled around the silent trees as we packed the car with the Christmas costumes and goodies for the children. The decorations had never been more beautiful. The children played their parts with enough enthusiasm and panache to more than disguise the fluffed lines and missed cues. Best of all, as I knelt to pray I could feel again the warmth and companionship of our church family, silently assuring me as we spoke and sang together that the real celebration had not been forgotten in a profit-hungry world.

I literally fell into bed exhausted at two a.m. on Christmas morning, having filled up the stockings and waited in the dark peace of our rambling house for Chris to return from the midnight service. Stella was still not home. I hoped she would be sober enough to climb the stairs.

At five-thirty Helen whooped into our bed to show us what Father Christmas had left for her, and to help us open our presents. Stella had not returned, I felt sure – a peep into the spare room confirmed my fears, as I saw the untouched bed and the bulging stocking.

At seven-thirty the phone rang. It was Stella, cheery as ever.

'Hallo, Beth. Merry Christmas. I hope I didn't wake you.'

Some chance.

'Where are you?' Relief at hearing her voice began to turn to anger. 'We were really worried.'

'I'm at the children's home, having breakfast.' Stella sounded surprised. 'Didn't I tell you I might stay over?'

'No, you didn't, young lady,' I spluttered. 'What's more, if you had done I would probably have said no. You can't just turn up on someone's doorstep and ask for a bed for the night.'

'You can here – they didn't mind, Beth, honestly.'

'I mind. Chris minds. Your bed is *here*!'

'Well sorry, then. But I really don't know what all the fuss is about. I'll probably be back tonight.'

'You most certainly will – and by midnight. This is not a hotel, you know.'

Oh, God. I shut my eyes and remembered my mother, who had blighted my teenage years with seemingly constant nagging. 'You treat this place like a hotel, not a home.' It had seemed so unreasonable: I had sworn never to say it.

'O.K. Beth. Merry Christmas.'

'Merry Christmas!' I slammed the phone down.

Helen was looking at me anxiously. 'Has Stella been naughty?'

'Oh, I don't know. I'm still half asleep.' I sank onto a chair. Helen advanced on me with one hand behind her back.

'I know what will cheer you up. You should pull a Christmas cracker,' she suggested hopefully. She drew out one which she had obviously pinched from the box hidden in my wardrobe.

'Helen! They're for lunch.'

'This looked like an extra one. And there might be something in it for me to play with.' She grinned, with the cunning of a true Reynard. 'It would keep me quiet for a bit.'

Helen I feel sure is destined to be a saleswoman – or a shop steward. I pulled her towards me as she flashed the smile of a winner. The ominous start to Stella's Christmas holiday was forgotten in the bliss of an old-fashioned tickle fight.

Christmas was over. The last of the turkey had been converted to curry, via sandwiches, pies and soups. We had consumed the last mouthful of Grandma's delicious pudding and finally given up on the Christmas cake, reserving the remains for such visitors as were not to be encouraged to stay for very long. When Ann telephoned to see how Stella was faring I realised we had in fact seen very little of her, though the hot water tank was completely drained every morning, and the bathroom occupied for two hours without fail.

'She seems to have had a great Christmas,' I said. 'We have just about reached a compromise – she does actually sleep in her bed here for some of the night. Otherwise she's out.'

'Well, I suppose it's only to be expected she'll go a bit wild after being cooped up. All the same, I hope she's not going off the rails again.'

'She can't be up to much, Ann. We've only given her a total of about fifteen pounds over Christmas week – that's not much these days when you are out on the town every night.'

'But what about the money I gave her before she came to you?'
Warning bells started to ring. 'What money?'

'I gave her forty-five pounds; thirty-five for a new coat and ten
pounds pocket money. Did she use it all on the coat?'

'No. No, she didn't,' I said slowly, 'because she didn't buy a
coat. She said you hadn't given her any money.'

There was a short silence, and then: 'Look, I'd better come
round and sort this out.'

I put down the telephone and went in search of Stella, who
happened to be making one of her rare appearances. When
challenged about the money, she said simply, 'Oh yes, I spent it. I
needed a night out more than I needed a new coat.'

'Stella, you spent more than sixty pounds in one week – on
what?'

'Living,' she pronounced.

'Living?'

'Living. Anyway, I haven't spent it all.' She searched her
pockets and triumphantly held up a pound note and fifty pence.

I toyed with the idea of a scathing retort, but in truth I couldn't
think of one. Only the things my mother had said to me:

'Money doesn't grow on trees, you know . . . when *I* was
young . . . you kids today don't know you're born . . .' They all
ran through my head. But what was the point? Save it, I thought.
She's only here another week. Leave it to Ann to sort out.

Social Workers have a reputation among many foster parents for
being weak and ineffective with teenagers; if so, Ann proved to be
the exception. Stella emerged from their hour-long session in our
living room thoroughly chastened.

'*She* says I can't have any more money 'til next week – *or* a
coat,' Stella mourned. Her wounded look had a tinge of hope in
it.

'Quite right, too,' I said unsympathetically. For a moment the
irrepressible Stella looked quite forlorn. Then she shrugged her
shoulders. 'Ah well. Easy come, easy go. I'll just have to do a little
wheeler-dealering.' She looked me straight in the eye as she spoke,
almost as though she was throwing out a challenge and expected
me to try and dissuade her.

'Serve her right,' I thought, 'if she *does* have to sell a precious
L.P. or whatever.' So I smiled the sort of over-sweet smile one
saves for such occasions and murmured, 'Yes, I suppose so.'

Poor, innocent fool. I should have known someone like Stella would not be in-to self-sacrifice.

'Can I use the phone?' she asked me just half an hour later.

'Yes, of course. I'm just popping round to the shops. Helen, Daddy is upstairs – don't disturb him unless you have to.'

'Right-o,' came the sticky reply through a mouthful of toffee. Stella again. I wondered if she had had a dental check-up recently.

When I returned, clutching the last minute odds and ends for the weekend, I found Stella still on the phone. Helen was sitting at the table, head cupped in hands, staring at her.

'Helen, don't be rude,' I said automatically, and began to unpack the shopping. Suddenly, stock cubes in hand, I was rooted to the spot as Stella's end of the conversation filtered through my pre-occupation with the evening meal.

'How much has he got? Well, tell him he can bring it all along – we can sell it dead easily. No, those made me sick – I passed them on to Cathy. Yeah, that's great – works fast, know what I mean? See you at Cathy's place, then. 'Bye . . .'

Stella was using our phone – the vicarage phone – to set up some sort of drugs deal!

'Chris!' I hissed as I entered the bedroom. Chris, still recovering from Christmas, was asleep in the armchair by the bed. Not that Chris will ever admit to sleeping during the day. 'Examining the inside of my eyelids,' *he* calls it. There was no response to my call. It has often bothered me that the children and I could be abducted, our furniture removed and the house burned down with Chris in it, and he would not turn a hair, so long as the perpetrators of these deeds chose a time when he was 'planning next week's sermon' or 'examining his eyelids'.

'Chris!' I poked him, and two unseeing blue eyes flashed open and then closed again. Drastic action was called for.

'Oh no . . .' I wailed. 'Chris, you didn't *want* these sermon notes did you?'

That woke him, and I explained Stella's latest exploit.

'And she doesn't see anything wrong in it,' I finished. 'She didn't so much as stop for breath when I came in – and all in front of Helen. You'd better go and speak to her, Chris.'

'*I'd* better . . .?'

'Yes. Coming in at night was mine. Drug pushing is yours.'

I shoved him towards the door. 'Go on. It's time to come the heavy with that young lady, however brief her stay, and don't be swayed by feminine charm or mock penitence,' I coached.

'Living with you has made me expert on feminine wiles,' said Chris sweetly.

'And while you're about it, see if there's any possibility of any of us being able to get into the bathroom in the mornings, or at least finding some hot water when we do. But don't let her sidetrack you from the main issue, or . . .'

'Look,' said Chris stonily. 'Why don't *you* deal with it?'

'Sorry.'

'Right. Over the top, men.' Chris flexed his biceps and marched down the stairs into battle.

'Well?' I greeted him later, having heard the front door close on our budding entrepreneuse.

'I told her,' he said.

'Told her what?'

'Not to use our phone for illicit purposes and especially not in front of Helen.'

'Illicit purposes?' I queried. 'Will she know what you mean?'

I began to suspect she had sidetracked him after all, but he neatly deflected my question with, 'She *said* she wasn't doing anything she hadn't told you about.'

He looked at me questioningly and I shook my head. 'I also told her how concerned we are about the whole thing, and about her, but she clearly thinks it's a fuss about nothing. She tells me she's not into anything real heavy, whatever that's supposed to mean. All we can do is talk to Ann – if Stella is to be believed, she knows all about this harmless little pursuit. After all, Stella is leaving next week. How can we get involved?'

I knew he was right but we both felt worried nonetheless. It was the first time we had come across this sort of problem; it seemed awfully calculating and callous to turn a blind eye simply because we might never see Stella again after a few days' time. I resolved, if possible, to find an opportunity to really have a talk with Stella.

This is one of the biggest dilemmas of fostering teenagers for a short time. You are becoming involved as 'parents' in a situation where your 'children' are virtual strangers. Delicate situations, where you might perhaps want to guide or advise, become even more delicate because you have no intimate knowledge or memory of each other which could provide a platform for frank discussion.

A mother will often know, instinctively, the best approach to her own child. A foster parent has to make a guess, and hope for the best.

In the end I did not have a chance to talk to Stella anyway. The next day we heard news that her flat was to be ready to move into in three days' time, and everyone was caught up in the excited preparations. Amidst all this, Stella had a hospital appointment to keep.

She was going through the long and painful process of having a tattoo removed from her arm ('Steve for me' was apparently part of her mis-spent youth, and was out of date anyway).

Chris took her to the hospital and sat with her in the waiting area. When Stella's turn came, the nurse who arrived to escort her

clearly had trouble placing the relationship between Stella and the young man in the conservative grey suit with a copy of *The Times* tucked under his arm. Her eyes travelled over Chris and then rested on Stella with a look of confusion. Finally, she asked, 'Do you want your boyfriend to come, too?'

Stella smiled broadly as Chris, red-faced, started to explain. 'Oh, no . . .'

Stella cut across him. 'No – he's far too squeamish.'

As she reached the door of the clinic, Stella turned and blew Chris a kiss, much to the amusement of the crowded waiting area.

'Bye bye, darling.'

This sort of confusion is rife in foster placements. I will never forget being called out in the night to the casualty department of our local hospital, after a sixteen-year-old foster daughter had suffered a broken ankle in an accident. They had asked if her mother would be at home and she, being too embarrassed to explain her situation, had said simply that she would. Her embarrassment was nothing to mine as, one by one, the medical staff involved peeped out from the cubicle where they were strapping the ankle to take a look at this incredibly young-looking mother (I was then twenty-four) and her gigolo boyfriend (Steve, our neighbour's son, had driven me to the hospital in his pyjamas). By the time I finally twigged *why* the staff were taking such an interest in us there was no point in explaining they had jumped to the wrong conclusions. I just collected the kid and the crutches and made for the exit.

Stella had one more surprise left for us. The day before she moved into her flat she introduced us to the new boyfriend. Less moronic than most, his name was Pete and he sported a bright blue Mohican-style stripe down the middle of his otherwise bald head. Helen could not take her eyes off him. Pete, it transpired, was the son of an eminent American theologian who was about to return to the States to take up a university position there. His family, naturally enough, was going to accompany him. Now, Stella had always fancied living abroad and regarded this as a heaven-sent opportunity. Chris and I listened open-mouthed as they told us their plans.

Stella and Pete, who had been dating for a week *but* who had known each other for, ooh, all of six months before Stella's departure to Croydon, were going to get married. As Pete's wife, they thought, Stella would have no visa problems. Once in the States, it would be easy enough to split up if they wanted to. 'A marriage of convenience,' Stella told us excitedly. 'We're going to do it on my eighteenth birthday – the day before we fly. Isn't it great?'

For some minutes we thought they were joking. But they were not. I could not believe my ears and sat dumb, not knowing what to say. One becomes so accustomed to greeting news of an engagement with exclamations of delight and congratulations. What *is* the appropriate response to an 'engagement of convenience'?

Chris, meanwhile, was refusing to believe Pete's parents would agree to such a charade. The 'sort-of' love birds agreed that Pete's dad was 'being a bit difficult', but were adamant that the final decision had been left up to Pete. Anyway, they argued, he would come round – in time.

The next day Stella left, leaving behind her only memories and a pile of empty bath oil containers. We never saw her again and we have no idea whether she made it to the United States of America and a new, married life. Our relief as she tootled off down the road on the back of Pete's motor bike, Ann and the luggage following behind in Ann's car, was enormous.

Now, several years later, we still laugh at Stella's antics and our own green-ness in those early days of fostering. Still, as we lie in bed or sit in the garden 'thinking of many things', one of us will punctuate the stillness with a chuckle.

'Hey,' we'll say. 'Remember the time when Stella . . .'

11

'What My Name?'

After Stella had left, Chris and I decided it was high time we caught up on all the things we had neglected during our past, very busy year of fostering. We seemed to have lived in constant upheaval. Now was the time to sort out all the chaos that had ensued from a large, ever changing family and no time for more than routine household chores.

I set about decorating the hall and stairs; no mean feat in a tall, Victorian house.

'There are thirty-nine steps in this house, which has to be significant,' I informed Chris gloomily after two solid hours of sanding had only dented the preparation that had to be done. 'There are thirty-nine steps, four landings, fourteen doors and miles of skirting board. It'll take me until I'm ninety.'

Chris, who hates decorating and always does his best to dissuade me from indulging in my greatest hobby, looked singularly unsympathetic: 'Your idea, not mine.'

I went back to work uncheered. The weather was cold and damp, not the best climate for drying paint. Helen drove me to distraction with her determination to be helpful. 'You missed a bit Mummy. No, there. . .there! I'll get it – whoops! Sorry, Mummy . . .' She also brought her friends round to have a look. 'Is it wet? Mmm, look, you can see your fingerprints. Ooh, my Mum'll kill me, it's my best dress . . .'

In the middle of all this we were asked to take a child. For the first time in four years I said, 'No'. We were determined to take no more children until the hall, the garden and Helen's room had been put to rights after long neglect, not to mention a good spring clean.

'Sorry,' I said. 'It just can't be done. I'm up to my eyeballs in paint and paper.'

It was as simple as that. No-one pushed or pressured, and I felt quite proud of my strong-mindedness. For three months I steadfastly refused even to hear any details of children coming into care. So how we came to have Jane – what factors were at work to make us weaken on that particular call, I just don't know.

Jane came into care suddenly, aged seven, when her mother was admitted to a mental hospital after a rather violent scene with the police. Jane was undersized, frightened, and mentally very retarded. Would we be able take her for a few weeks, while a long-term home was found?

'I've heard you are not really taking anyone on at the moment,' said a tired voice at the other end, 'but I've tried just about everything else.'

Such a child is never easy to find a place for. Chris and I both felt we had no good reason to refuse, although we were not tremendously keen.

'We can do it for a couple of months at the most,' I said. 'Then we have family coming to stay and things will be very busy.'

'We'll do our best to fix something up by then. Thanks – thanks a lot.'

Within the hour Jane was on our doorstep. She was indeed tiny – and shivering with cold. She wore shorts, plimsolls and a T-shirt. Her social worker, Anna, had wrapped her own jacket around her, but Jane was not by any means dressed for a chilly day in March.

'Hallo, Jane,' I smiled.

I got a very timid grin from the freckled face, and beckoned her over nearer to the fire. Anna explained that Jane had been kept in virtual isolation from other people ever since she was a baby. School, friends, toys, anything to do with the outside world had been fiercely resisted by her mother, whose acute illness made her fearful of anything outside her front door. Jane had received virtually no stimulation except for the television: as far as we could gather it had been on every waking moment, and had fed Jane her view and perception of life.

Since Jane had almost no speech, she could understand very little of what we were saying. I noticed that Anna smiled at her encouragingly from time to time, and kept the tone of her voice deliberately light even as she told us the horrific details of Jane's life at home. Jane responded to any attention with a coy grin which grew broader and warmer by the minute.

'It's impossible to say how much of Jane's handicap is genetic and how much a result of her treatment. So we'll have to see what happens now that she has a more stimulating environment.'

'Clothes?' I queried.

Anna grimaced. 'None that you would want to put her in. She has not been *deliberately* neglected or ill-treated, as far as we can tell. But her mother is so sick . . . well, she never bought clothes. When we got into the place, with the police, it was not the most sanitary of houses. I couldn't find anything except these rags – no coat, even. So we'll rush a clothing grant through. I'm afraid all she has are the clothes she has on and these.'

'These' were three tin bricks in a wooden box – the only plaything Jane possessed. It was hardly credible, in wealthy Britain, that all this had escaped the notice of an army of health visitors, teachers, doctors and so on. Surely *someone* must have known. But there was no point in pursuing spilt milk now. (Later, we discovered that Jane had actually been under some sort of supervision order, and that Anna had visited quite regularly. But there had been no cast-iron case for removing Jane from the home, and while there was still hope of keeping mother and child together, Anna had battled on.)

'Would you like a drink, Jane?' Chris asked.

Jane nodded her head warily.

'Juice? Milk?'

'Mik.'

Chris poured some milk. Jane drank thirstily, and took the biscuit Helen offered her.

'You're sharing a bedroom with me. Want to see?'

Again Jane nodded. Helen held out her hand and they went off together.

It was decided that, with the Easter break coming up anyway, Jane would not be sent to school while she was with us. No-one knew where she would be finally placed – a national advertisement was being run in The National Foster Care Association's magazine. It was pointless enrolling her in a school she would not be able to settle in, and so these few weeks were to be devoted to providing pleasant, stimulating experiences. It sounded like a real challenge, and Chris and I felt enthusiastic. Whatever we did would have to be valuable – Jane was almost a classic *tabula rasa* with no experiences of anything much. A Sunday roast, a book, clothes of her own – all these would be new experiences.

In the next couple of days we got down to the business of finding out how much Jane could do. It seemed she was very independent in terms of survival skills – she could dress herself, use a knife and fork, go to the loo and so on. But her speech was about the same as Helen's had been at eighteen months, and most of her conversation consisted of a shake of the head or 'No me know'. Jane did not know her age or her full name; she could neither write nor recognise even the initial 'J'. Nor did she know any colours, except 'pak' pointing to a black counter which appeared to be her favourite.

Chris and I were staggered at how much Jane did not know. We could not begin to comprehend what life must be like for her, what she thought was going on around her. Yet Jane did seem to understand at least the gist of what was said to her very well indeed. It was lack of vocabulary that thwarted her – Jane had simply not had the chance to learn words like 'ice cream' or 'salt and pepper'. Even 'shoes' and 'elbow' meant nothing. She looked absolutely floored when I asked her if she would like a fork or a spoon at dinner on that first evening. She knew what each item was by sight, but could not recall, if she had ever known, what they were called. It is difficult to describe the sort of things Jane could not say or do, and as I look back now I still wonder how on earth she managed to survive at all.

One word Jane knew very well – 'telly'. She glued herself to it at every possible opportunity, regardless of what was showing.

On her second day with us, I took Jane and Helen out to buy new clothes. While Helen went to roam through the track suits – the only clothes she could be induced to take an interest in – I bought Jane a complete stock of underwear, socks, two dresses, dungarees and a coat. All were sized 'four/five years', although Jane would be eight in a few months time.

Jane was totally bewildered by all these possessions, and did not like the shoes we bought at all, at first. She said, 'themfunny', meaning they felt strange after the plimsolls, which we discovered were two sizes too small as well as being badly worn. Jane's toes are permanently deformed.

The coat, though was a big success. It was bright red, and we
bought gloves to match. Jane could hardly contain her excitement
– she had seen gloves before, but never owned any. Once on, they
stayed on for days, even at meal times. She surrendered the gloves
only at bath time, and watched them carefully even then, fearful
they would be snatched away from her.

Jane was very timid at first. She shrank from raised voices and
was over-obedient, stumbling over herself in her anxiety to please.
She was terrified if she thought we were cross with her. We could
not know what had happened to her at home – there were no signs
of physical abuse. Indeed, her mother appeared to have been very
fond of her, and was constantly telling the Social Worker who
visited her in hospital how much she looked forward to getting
better, and having Jane back. But her mother's terrible illness and
psychotic delusions made this almost an impossibility. Mean
while, a legacy of enormous handicap had been bequeathed to her
child. To me, the fact that her mother had genuine love for Jane
even while she was treating her as though she hated her, make
their situation all the more tragic; it does not provide any comfort

Somewhere, though, Jane had managed to hold on to the tiny seed of her own personality, and as time wore on a cheerful, sunny disposition emerged. Within a couple of days, Jane was chattering away non-stop – complete rubbish to us, since it was all baby-talk, but if you concentrated hard you could just about get the message.

Food was the first focal point of her life, after television. Jane loved sausages and chips, familiar from her old home. Her first experience of chocolate made her grimace; she preferred crisps. It was our family that contributed that particular taste to Jane's development. Regrettably for her teeth, she learned to like it very quickly.

Jane and Helen formed an immediate bond. Communication held no problems for them. They spent whole days in the school holidays in their room, emerging for drinks and snacks that would be borne away with much conspiratorial giggling. Within three weeks, Jane had outgrown all her new clothes and we had to buy more. Her growth was phenomenal – you really could almost *see* it. And she learnt fast, too.

Day after day, hour after hour, we all played a board game which involved throwing a dice to collect coloured balls in a particular order. These were then threaded on to a stick, the winner being the one to complete the sequence. I have the game tucked away in the attic to this day, to prove that we actually wore it out. I hope never to play it again. Chris and I became absolutely sick of the sight of it, and would groan whenever Jane reached for the shelf where it sat. But the girls loved it, and our efforts were well rewarded. By the time Helen went back to school, Jane could count to five and knew the primary colours, as well as white and green. Her speech was rapidly improving, and we decided to concentrate on that.

Jane found names very difficult, both to recall and to pronounce, even her own. It seemed important to start there.

'Hallo there – who are you?' I would ask when she came into the room.

'Uh . . . No me know. What my name?'

'Come on, *you* know.'

There would be a long pause while she screwed up her face.

'Oh, 'es, it Dane.'

'Jane.'

'Dane.'

'J . . .J . . .Jane. You try it.'
'J . . .J . . .Dane.', and so on.
And so on and so on. Everybody was talking, from morning to
night, repeating words and phrases over and over for Jane's
benefit – conversation at the meal table became like an inter-
national convention of talking snails with work-to-rule interpre-
ters. Luckily, just before it drove me mad, Chris began to take an
especial interest in Jane's speech therapy, and took over the
responsibility for going with her to intensive sessions at the local
Health Centre. Chris had not had much opportunity to use his
Honours degree in cognitive psychology in the parish, but the
experience came into its own now. He spent hours recording
Jane's developing speech, and thinking of games which would
identify the problems and work on them. My contribution became
more or less that of a parrot, repeating back whatever Jane said to
me. If she had spoken correctly, it was reinforced by hearing it
again; if she had made a mistake, she heard it properly said. The
improvement of Jane's speech with all this attention was remark-
able, but it is impossible to convey how wearing it all was.
    Anna visited us regularly, sometimes twice a week, forming that
essential link between the two homes. She was able to reassure
Jane that her mother was all right, and that she loved her. Simple
messages were conveyed, and Anna and Jane started off a 'life
story' scrapbook together that would ensure Jane's roots were with
her even after social workers and memories had faded. In the book
they pasted a photograph of Mum, standing outside the old home.
Anna wrote down little snippets of Jane's past, whatever they
could remember between them, good and bad. They included the
traumatic evening when Jane had been taken into care, with Anna
gently encouraging Jane to describe to Chris and I what had
happened. Then *we* took over the scrapbook, recording our
outings and doings as a family. Jane has the book still; it is a
treasured possession.
    As soon as Jane was settled, I began concentrated efforts to get
her to hold a pencil and begin the basics of reading and writing. I
bought dozens of pre-reading workbooks, picture books, story
tapes – anything that seemed helpful. I took out a monthly account
with the Early Learning Centre, who sent wonderful packages
through the post, both for Jane and for Helen, so that she would
not feel left out. Together we traced miles and miles of curly lines,

matched pairs of socks and helped countless little doggies find their way through countless mazes to their kennels. I made Jane's name out of paper, plasticine, sandpaper, anything I could get my hands on. Here again, there was progress. It took Jane a week to be able to recognise her name among others written on a sheet, another to copy it neatly, and a month later she was writing it by herself with confidence.

Helen was unwittingly our most invaluable teaching tool: Jane watched, and copied. I was amazed at Helen, usually so quickfire, so impatient with anyone who could not keep up with her. Her patience with her new foster sister was boundless. I have never experienced such persistence in her – before or since!

'It's your turn, Jane – throw the dice.'

They would sit there for a good couple of minutes while Jane counted two dots. She was invariably wrong anyway. I had to give up playing board games with Jane – this slowness and backtracking set my teeth on edge. But Helen just carried on regardless. 'No, it's three – see? One, two, three. Now move the counter. Look, this way; no, this way. Good.' Another two minutes and Helen would get her turn; a few seconds later it was back to waiting. Helen is no angel and can be a real trial, like any child. But I was filled with admiration for the way she took Jane under her wing and stuck to the task. Slowly but surely, Jane's recognition and use of numbers improved.

'Mummy, come and see this!' said Helen one day. She led me upstairs where Jane sat absorbed in a puzzle. It was an eighty-piece 'Mr Man' jigsaw. Helen, who had no patience for such things, had discarded it without ever completing it. Jane, however, was half way through and determined not to give up until it was finished. Her powers of concentration were enormous, comparable to any intelligent adult's.

Excitedly, we dug out other puzzles. Jane could do them all; some she could complete more quickly than I.

'It's as though her visual memory has become super-developed to compensate for not having language,' I told Anna. 'You know, like blind people having better touch or smell. She can sew, too. I've taught her a couple of simple stitches and she does it all so neatly – streets ahead of Helen.'

'That's great news, Beth,' said Anna. 'But how's she getting on as part of the family?'

'It's a lot of work', I admitted, 'and very frustrating sometimes. If you're in a hurry she gets confused and slows right down, or she forgets what she's supposed to be doing. There's all sorts of things like that which are really frustrating and make you want to throw something at her, poor child. And yet – we can't remember what life was like without her. She and Helen get on so well . . .'

'Beth,' interrupted Anna. 'I'm asking because there has been no response to our advertisement.'

'What, none?'

'No serious enquiries.'

'But surely . . .'

Anna shrugged. 'Usually these methods pay off. But think about it. *You* say she's cute and sweet and has no behaviour problems. Looked at from the outside, she's a seven-year-old kid with a severe mental handicap whose mother's a nutter. That's how people who don't know her base their judgement. Not many people are willing to take on that. It's a risk to their own family set-up, if you know what I mean.'

Chris and I had already realised that it would be no easy task finding Jane a new home. We had discussed at great length what we would do if no permanent place could be found in another foster family. We were very wary of taking on another long-term child ourselves, especially after Roger and Karen. But we were beginning to absorb Jane into the family, and time would only tighten the bond.

'Look, Anna – Chris and I *might* be able to keep her,' I said hesitantly. 'That is, keep trying. I mean, we don't feel very sure about it. Quite honestly, the thought of dealing with that level of mental handicap, day after day after day, scares me half to death, not to mention all the other problems which will come when she gets to be a teenager, and then an adult. But still, we are growing very fond. All of us.'

Anna collected her things together and stood up to get her coat. 'It's not something to do lightly, you know. She's coming on in leaps and bounds, we can all see that. She may go far. Already she's a completely different child. But no-one can say what will happen.'

'I know, I know,' I said. 'She could reach the end of what she can accomplish any time. We understand all that. That's why I say keep trying to find her a home. But – look, Anna – don't settle for anything less than *we* can give her. We want her to have more, not less. O.K.?'

Anna patted my shoulder and left without saying any more. I knew she understood our commitment to her little client, and also our hesitation. Over the years, we were to get to know each other very well, Anna and I. We fought often, arguing fiercely over many issues. She and Helen did not get along at all, and Helen behaved appallingly whenever Anna made a call on us. Chris did not take to her strongly analytical approach to the tasks in hand. Nonetheless, we all respected her.

Anna was a true, caring professional. She remained Jane's field worker for five full years, something of a record in our experience. She was a bridge between the old life and the new, an important link to Jane's past. Anna did much to overcome the physical and emotional obstacles to making Jane truly one of the family.

For of course, Jane never left us. Three months after her first arrival we committed ourselves to a new daughter. Jane started learning a new surname, and we had photographs taken.

I have them still. The little freckled face, with its monkey grin and gappy teeth, takes its place quite comfortably among the rest of the family. Jane is now a teenager, prone to spots and sulks like any other. Sometimes, when she is particularly moody and I would like to throttle her, I pull out those early photographs and remind myself of those first few years. And even while I rant and rave at Jane's mulish obstinacy or laziness, I never fail to thank God for sending her to us.

12

One Daughter, Delivered to our Door

Once Jane had taken her place as truly one of the family, there was much discussion about future plans. Anna felt very strongly that we should give up fostering altogether. She argued that Jane would always need so much attention that we would not be able to give her our best, with other children around. While Chris and I could see the point of this, we could also see the drawback of all family attention being focussed on Jane; after all, we did have another child already. And Jane, we felt, was not only able to cope with lots of things going on around her, she actually seemed to be stimulated and excited by them. Besides, fostering had become a way of life we were used to. We were loath to give up completely, and wanted to get Jane settled and then get back into the fray. But could we count on being able to settle Jane properly if we were taking in other children for short periods? So the arguments went, round and round. In the end, we made it known that we would take no more children for at least six months. After that, we would see how things were going. In any case, we would have to be very choosy about the sort of child we would take in the future.

Meanwhile, Jane's store of happy experiences continued to grow, feeding her mind and oiling the wheels of all the sleepy parts of her brain. Her birthday party – the first birthday she had ever celebrated – was to be the crowning glory in all this. Jane already had some idea of what should happen at such an event. Helen's birthday was just a month before her own. Jane had observed, with great enjoyment, the twenty or so bopping eight year olds who had bundled into our house for the occasion. She was too scared to join in any of the games, but had proudly looked after the prizes and fetched and carried from the kitchen.

By this time we had settled Jane into a small infants school near
to home. Although she was two years older than her classmates,
Jane was still small enough to blend in perfectly. She was to have
one year of schooling there before a proper educational assessment
was sought. It was very difficult to test Jane's abilities accurately
because of the complete lack of input in her early years. Chris and
I were hopeful that, given the speed with which she had learned
with us at home, by the time the year was through Jane would be
able to cope in the remedial department of a normal junior school.
We were working towards this goal with all our might and main.
Everything became a learning tool, even party invitations.

'So, who do you want to come to your party?' I said, pen poised
over the invitation list. I knew Jane would have to try very hard to
put a name to the faces that entered her mind.

'You,' she said.

'Yes, I'm coming already, darling. Otherwise who would feed
you all?'

'Oh,' a shy giggle. 'Ellin.'

'Helen.'

'Ellen, 'es.'

'Well, Helen's coming too.'

I knew Jane; by the time we had gone through the entire
extended family we could be here all night.

'Children from school, Jane. Who do you want to come from
your class?'

Jane thought about this for a long time. Then her face
brightened. She held up three fingers.

'Three children?'

''es.'

'Right. What are their names?'

Jane counted them off. 'Girl wiv pak 'air. Boy gotta bad 'and.
Girl sitta next me.'

'I need their names, darling, to write on the envelope. Can you
remember *any* of the names?'

Mournfully, Jane shook her head. This was a typical example of
the sort of thing taken for granted with a normal eight year old.
Every single thing was beset with complications where Jane was
involved. At least this one was easy to resolve. After a quiet word
with Jane's teacher, I wrote out twelve invitations to the children
she played with at school.

The great day arrived. The food was ready, the music played, and Jane sat in high anticipation, proudly arranging her party dress like a queen with her stately robes. The magic hour was three o'clock.

At twenty to three the first guest arrived – a little boy named Georgie. The bandage identified him as 'boy gotta bad 'and'. Georgie was newly arrived from Cyprus and did not speak a word of English, so when I asked him how he had hurt his hand he just smiled pleasantly, and eyed the cheese and pineapple.

What do you do with a child who arrives twenty minutes early for a birthday party? It seemed out of keeping with the festive atmosphere to leave him sitting there, and conversation was not going to be easy. So, I suddenly decided that we needed two parcels for 'pass-the-parcel' instead of one, and Georgie was put to work wrapping up a toy clown to fit on the end of a pencil.

'He knows what's in it, now,' said Helen. 'That's not fair – he'll tell everybody!'

'Helen,' I gave her a withering look 'Do *you* know the Greek for "little toy clown that goes on the end of the pencil"?'

Helen looked puzzled for a moment. Then 'Oh,' she said.

'Cunning, huh?' I asked triumphantly.

With a weary look, Helen took up her position next to Jane at the window. Clever mothers are such a bore.

At three o'clock, we were waiting for that first ring on the doorbell. At ten past three we were still waiting. At half past I said brightly, 'Well, perhaps we should play a game? Or even eat?'

Jane silently shook her head. It was one of the most awful moments of my life. Her very first party, the long anticipated sequel to Helen's extravaganza was about to be a dismal fizzle.

'Mummy, you must have put the wrong day on,' accused Helen.

'Darling, I didn't, honestly. Anyway, Georgie is here.'

'What can we *do*?' I hissed at twenty-to-four.

'Go out to the highways and byeways, and compel them to come in,' intoned Chris.

'Typical, Vicar. This is not time to quote the Bible at me – *do* something.'

'In other words, Beth, get on the phone upstairs and rally the neighbours round – and get our families to come now instead of tonight. Get anyone who can be here fast.'

It was an idea that saved the party, though I don't know what Georgie must have thought of this first experience of an English child's birthday.

Jane, for whom every day was a complex puzzle that had to be sorted, simply assumed that she had misunderstood what was supposed to happen, and she had a great time with all the 'surprise' guests.

This setback made us all the more determined that Jane's first Christmas celebrations would be extra-special. And they were. Jane was as captivated and bewildered as any toddler. Father Christmas was coming – and to her! She was determined to stay awake, and had a lot more will power than Helen. It was well after midnight before Chris could don his red suit and beard (we always go the whole hog in our family) and tiptoe in with the loaded stockings.

That Christmas was full of colour and sound and scent, lingering in the memory. It was a family tradition to buy, each year, one new special bauble. A white satin ribbon would be attached, upon which we would write the single most important or memorable event of the preceding year. This year Jane watched proudly as a bright red-glass sphere with a gold star in the centre of it, marked simply 'Jane' and the year, was hung beside 'Helen'. There could be no doubt now that Jane was a card-carrying member of the Miller family.

The New Year, however, brought disappointment. Jane's school report was gloomy. She was still way behind even the five-year-olds in reading and number skills. The headmistress felt it was only right to warn us that it was unlikely Jane would gain enough ground to avoid a special school by the time summer term ended.

We had already suspected this for ourselves, but it was still disappointing to see it in stark black and white. Jane had reached a plateau. All that she could absorb in that first year she had done. Now, with a mental age of about four, it was going to be a long, hard, slog.

At home, Jane continued to be timid and over-eager to please, but she would blossom almost visibly when any attention was paid to her. She was kind, very sweet-natured, and loved helping around the house and feeling needed. The highest compliment for Jane has always been, to this day, 'Oh Jane, you're such a help – what would I do without you?' This is guaranteed to make her glow with pride and dash off to sweep the stairs or make 'a nice cuppa tea'.

Of course, life was not all roses and sweet smiles. Her very slowness made Jane thoroughly irritating to be with after a time, and I dreaded having her at home all day on her own when Helen and Chris were both gone. Her inertia as she sat and watched every move I made would set me on edge, and I would have to constantly think of things for her to do while I got on with the housework, because I simply could not bear this totally silent, absolutely still little person staring at me, hour after hour. It was spooky after a short lifetime of Helen's persistent chatter. But Jane just loved to watch what I was doing, and had no concentration left over for words.

The one single thing that has remained the most difficult facet of caring for Jane, as well as hampering her own progress, is a complete inflexibility. Once something has been learned and absorbed it is immovable. Instructions are taken literally. You have to be very, very careful what you say, and we are all constantly caught out. When, for instance, I told Jane that she must not open a new bottle of milk every time she wanted a drink, Jane nodded solemnly.

'Use the opened milk,' I repeated.

''es, all right.'

The next day Jane came to me in high indignation. 'Oo done *dis*?' She pointed to a bottle of milk I had opened. She had absorbed the instruction not to open a new bottle of milk so well that she would not even start a new bottle when all the opened ones were used up. Another time, when Jane had a friend over to play, I said, 'You can go in your bedroom or the living room, but not in the study – I've got all my work laid out in there.'

Jane nodded happily enough and went off to play. Imagine my horror then, when her little friend came downstairs covered in 'Tippex' from my desk, clutching a creased-up bunch of papers in her hand which turned out to be the magazine article I had slaved over and typed out ready to send to the Editor. It had taken me hours and was now useless: grubby, crumpled, it bore the definite art work of a five-year-old hand.

Furious, I asked Jane what on earth she thought she had been doing. 'I told you not to go into the study, you naughty little girl!' I yelled.

Jane's bottom lip trembled. 'I not go in.'

'What's all this then?' I brandished my poor brain-child under her nose.

'Shawon did it.'

'But what was Sharon doing in the study in the first place?' I asked.

Jane looked puzzled. 'You not say *Shawon* not go in . . .'

Not realising the plural meaning of 'you', Jane had stood at the door of the study and watched while Sharon roamed around playing with whatever took her fancy.

Then there was the time Chris's mother asked me why Jane was not allowed to eat biscuits. It seemed unfair, she pointed out, to refuse Jane and not Helen, who had been merrily chomping away all afternoon while on a visit to Grandma's house.

'I've never said she can't eat biscuits,' I said, totally confused. Finally, after a piece of detection work worthy of the great Hercule Poirot, we traced it to the previous week, when Jane had asked if she could have a biscuit. I was preparing the evening meal at the time. 'No,' I said, 'Because you won't eat dinner if you have a biscuit now.' Apparently, Jane had it firmly fixed in her mind that if she were to eat a biscuit – any biscuit, anywhere – she would not be allowed to have dinner that night.

This sort of thing was a constant headache, and we were a bit worried about the wider implications for Jane, especially as she got older and more independent. We mentioned it to the Educational Psychologist when Jane finally came up for assessment.

'Oh yes, that's quite a common problem with mentally handicapped people,' he told us blithely.

It was the first time we had heard the label 'mentally handicapped' applied to our Jane, and it did not seem to suit her. She *looked* so bright, so alert, not at all like other mentally

handicapped people we had come into contact with. Surely she
would catch up, one day?

The psychologist shook his head. 'I'm awfully sorry, there's no
possibility. The average I.Q. is 100 – Jane's is . . .well, I would
put a maximum of 50 to it. You have to prepare yourself for her
never being able to live a fully independent life.'

He could see that this came as a shock, and tactfully leafed
through his papers for a moment while Chris and I absorbed the
news.

'Jane has made marvellous progress,' he went on, 'even in the
couple of months I have been observing her, there has been visible
improvement. Her social skills will carry on developing, I hope,
while she has such a caring and helpful home. But, I'm afraid she
is severely sub-normal, and as far as education goes Jane will need
a special school.'

'Will she read and write fluently, one day?' I asked hopefully.
We could not imagine what life would be like for her if she were
completely illiterate. Please, I thought, at least let her be able to
read the newspaper headlines, or a letter from a friend, or an
address – a bus destination – anything.

The psychologist shrugged. 'She will recognise a few words,
perhaps. Read? No, not as you and I understand the term.'

My heart sank to rock bottom. We had experienced a few
disappointments with our various children; this was the worst of
them all. It seemed, then, like a sentence of life-long hopelessness.
And Jane was not even nine years old.

Funnily enough, although we had fought tooth and nail against
such a prognosis, and it had been our greatest fear over the past
year, the more we thought about it, the less it seemed to matter
after all.

'She's happy and sweet-tempered,' we told each other. 'She's
instantly lovable, and there'll always be someone willing to give
her a hand with the things she can't manage . . .'

In the back of our minds we knew this could be hopelessly
optimistic. But what else could we do? Jane was a part of us, come
what may.

Helen and Jane grew closer and closer together. Within a year,
Jane had outstripped Helen in growth and was almost normal size
for her age. Added to this she was very strong and wiry.

The two formed, in time, a 'brain and brawn' agreement. Helen explained this to me soon after I saw a little boy fleeing from the local park as I arrived to meet the girls. He claimed that 'loony', the 'spasticko' had belted him. Helen confirmed this.

'But only because he was being horrid, Mummy. Sometimes the children tease Jane because she can't speak properly. *That* boy said she's a spastic and a nut case, and wears nappies. I tried to explain that *actually* she is mentally handicapped, which is not the same thing at all.' I could well imagine it. Helen, brought up on regular doses of her father's sermons and pronouncements, can be awfully pompous – and long-winded – when she has a bee in her bonnet.

'That was very good of you, Helen,' I said. 'But what happened?'

'He wouldn't listen,' she said calmly, with the indifferent shrug of a Chicago gangster. 'So I told Jane to hit him.'

Part of me felt there was something not quite Christian in this approach. But he had been a particularly nasty-looking little boy, so I said nothing. After all, as a mother I had to encourage them to make their own way in the world, didn't I?

It was really the growing relationship between the two girls that made Chris and I decide it was time to give up fostering. We did not want to risk the closeness that Jane and Helen had forged. Also, to be truthful, we had come to appreciate the peaceful, normal life of a small family. When I was offered the opportunity of a part-time teaching job which would fit in well with the children, the decision was sealed. It was back to the real, sane world for us all.

With regret, we told our social worker that we would be taking no more children, and wanted our name removed from their register of foster parents kept by the local authority.

'At least,' I found myself saying quite by accident, 'for the forseeable future.' I met Chris's gaze as I put down the phone.

'Well, that's it, Chris. A chapter of our life closed. We shall never foster another child.'

Chris put his arm around me and bent to whisper in my ear.

'What, never?'

'No, never.'

'What, never?'

I smiled. 'Well, hardly ever . . .'

Epilogue

From the very beginning, Chris and I decided that we would not actively maintain contact with any of our foster children. It was hard, not knowing whether things were working out as everyone had hoped, wondering how they were celebrating their birthdays, whether such-and-such a baby was walking yet, and so on. Nonetheless, we felt that we were a passing phase in the lives of these children, especially the little ones. It would be confusing for them and perhaps threatening for their parents, if we tried to stay in touch. And anyway, it could even be more painful than not knowing. What could we do, after all, if the family hit another bad patch, except watch and suffer with them? We could not be constantly on call for an ever-growing number of children. So good-bye was, for us, always final.

On the other hand, where teenagers were concerned, who were old enough to choose for themselves, we left it up to them whether or not they returned. We always made a point of telling them they would be welcome, but did not push them to visit us.

Glen returned a couple of times, and eventually came to live in our area, so we often had a casual conversation in the High Street. Stella disappeared without a trace. Perhaps she is an American housewife now, with growing children of her own. Somehow I doubt it. Roger phoned us once, a week after he left, and then there was silence.

For over a year we heard nothing from Karen. Then a solicitor came to see us. Karen and Wayne were back together, and expecting another child. They were going to court, to try and have Tina returned to them. As the people who had been most closely involved, we were asked to comment on Karen's ability to cope.

Chris and I were horrified. Although Karen was now almost

eighteen, we could not believe she was able to cope with the stress of two small children. Tina was now two years old, the great tantrum age. Add a new-born baby? I actually had nightmares about it. Reluctantly, we swore an affidavit detailing the events after Tina's birth, saying very strongly that we felt Karen would not be able to take on such a responsibility, and that Tina would almost certainly be at risk if she were uprooted from the Holroyds and returned to Wayne and Karen.

I visited their new home in a neighbouring borough, clutching a copy of the affidavit. It was an encounter I dreaded, but if we were to be on opposite sides of a court battle, I at least wanted to tell them how sorry we were about it. I expected to be thrown out on my ear. It is a great tribute to Karen and Wayne, who were still little more than kids themselves, that I was not. Karen read out the statement, listened to my stumbling apology, and said, 'You're only doing what you think is best for Tina, and us. I can understand that – I'm glad you still care that much about us.'

So we were re-united, not as a family but as friends. To our surprise, Karen and Wayne won the court case. Tina was to be returned, after a series of visits, although contact with the Holroyds would be maintained. We were sad, anxious, and thoroughly disillusioned with legal processes.

Today, Tina is at school, and her little brother is growing fast. We visit each other now and then, and spend some of Christmas together each year. Never have we been more delighted to be proved wrong.

Four years after Karen and Roger left, we answered the door one evening to find a strange young man. He was very tall, slim, with long hair and casually elegant clothes. He smiled at us.

'Hallo. Remember me?'

We were at a loss. *I* had certainly never seen him before. It must be one of the many con tricks we had been subjected to while living in the city. It would end, no doubt, in a request for money.

'No,' we said.

The smile became a grin, a cloak of self-assured charm thrown over natural shyness. That grin had often infuriated me.

'Roger?' I asked incredulously. 'Are *you* – Roger?'

Indeed he was. The school we had so doubtingly entrusted him to had, it seemed, found his potential after all. He was a Sixth-former, studying towards University. And in need of a home now that his Grandmother was going to live abroad.

It must have taken a good deal of courage to turn up out of the blue like that, and with such a request. We had not parted on very encouraging terms. Yet Roger must have felt some of the bond we had felt, or why was he here, and not pestering his Social Worker to find him a little flat of his own, or a room in a hostel?

Roger lodged with us for a year; a time not without its problems, particularly after I discovered, to my joy, that we were at last going to have another child of our own. (It was one of Roger's basic contentions, throughout the sickness, the sleepless nights, and the yo-yo swings of emotion, that I, having a University degree, should be able to counteract all these symptoms. Myself, I never understood what the connection was!) In many ways, Roger was the same vulnerable, infuriating and immature boy we had said goodbye to four years previously. When he left, we encouraged him to stay in touch. Hopefully he is at University now, but I have no idea where he is. I may well have to wait a few years for a letter, or a card. Such is Roger, such is life as a foster parent: in a nutshell, the most frustrating, heartbreaking, exhilarating and rewarding life-style imaginable. Success is great. But success in fostering is special; it comes from being able to live with failure without letting it sap your confidence. It is being able to say goodbye forever to a child you have grown to love, and welcome a small stranger, all in the space of a couple of days. People ask us, 'How can you do it – how can you let them go?' Well, sometimes it is hard, of course. On the other hand, you know from the start that these children are not staying with you permanently. Much as you might do when a favourite niece or nephew – or grandchild perhaps – comes to stay, you make the most of the time you have with them, and surrender them up to their rightful homes when the time comes.

Cases of children growing up in a foster family and being torn, suddenly and unexpectedly, from the arms of the mother they have come to love and trust, make good copy and are well publicised. Such cases are, fortunately, rare, and not to be feared (although all foster parents will, I think, have had just this sort of anxiety at the back of their minds at some time).

The experiences bequeathed to the members of the fostering triangle – the child, the natural parents and the foster parents – are always different. Fostering is a sort of very complicated geometry. There *is* a structure and a pattern to it, somewhere in the maze of conflicts, efforts, rewards and failures, but it is not a pattern easily explained to those who don't know it first-hand. The view from each corner of the fostering triangle must differ. I cannot speak for the natural parents of a child in care, except to say I wish I knew more about what actually happens to them when they see their children taken and looked after by complete strangers. The children themselves are surprisingly resilient, and our own experience as foster parents you have shared in the pages of this book.

Fostering is just a part of a great web of Social Services facilities provided for child care. In the past, all those local authority bodies and government departments that we ordinary folk refer to as the great 'they' have not lavished much attention on foster care. But this attitude was changing even as we began our fostering career, and there has been a real blossoming of foster care with it being seen as the best option for increasing numbers of children. These include the mentally and physically handicapped, and disturbed teenagers, who were traditionally seen as automatic no-no's.

Foster care is much, much cheaper than running institutions with full-time staff and all the attendant costs. But of course the benefits are not counted in money terms alone. Foster care gives children caught in conflict the experience of a happy family life. They see, perhaps for the first time, that adults *do* trust and care for each other, and that anger does not always mean physical violence. Hopefully, they slowly begin to believe that they themselves are worthy of love, even if their own parents do not want them. So many children 'in care' feel they must have done something terribly wrong, for which they are being punished or sent away. Or that they are simply not 'good' or loveable enough.

Family care is something taken for granted by too many of us. Picture the teenage girl who has spent her life in a children's home. Not for her the privacy of her own room. She may never even have known the simple pleasure of an hour alone in the house, with a favourite television programme. The intimate details of her life are passed on, in a paper file, to whoever deals with her 'case'. Her parents are whichever residential workers happen to be on duty at the time. They are loving, caring people. But they change two or three times a day, and many move on to a different job after two or three years. And this will be the experience on which she must base her own idea of family life when she marries and has children of her own.

Horrifying? We thought so, many years ago when we watched a then-revolutionary documentary about children in care. It ended with an appeal by the children themselves, for foster families. It stuck in our minds. It was several years, though, before we tentatively approached our Town Hall to 'find out about fostering'. Twenty or so foster children later, we have never regretted that decision. I don't deny that it is hard to take another mother's child. It *is* hard to deal with your foster child's own roots, the pull of a family you may never ever meet, or whose life style you deeply disapprove of or can never understand. But the foster parent is the one with the power of escape, the only one who has no legal or even moral obligation to go on past the point of endurance.

Natural parents have a tendency to become the villains of the piece when it comes to children going into care. However, many of the parents of children in care love their children, mind very much, and want to do their best for them. For one reason or another, they are just unable to cope. Stress, illness, marital breakdown: all kinds of things can be heaped and piled up until the family reaches breaking point and needs at least a breathing space, if not a complete rescue service.

If you take on the responsibility for the day-to-day care of such a child, you also take on the anxiety of a parent or parents who do not know you and may not trust you. They will be encouraged to visit their children, and will have to arrange all that with you, a stranger. They may well feel humiliated and almost certainly acutely embarrassed that you, having all the luck, can provide a stable home while they, however hard they fight to, cannot.

Frankly, it can be embarrassing to the foster parent too. I wonder how *I* would cope if someone took from me my husband, home and income, and squashed me into substandard housing, and blessed me with depressive illness. The fact is, I did not go out into the world actively *seeking* a pleasant birthplace, a good education, the 'right' man and a secure environment. They were not my just reward for years of toil and struggle; they just about fell into my lap. I'm lucky; it's as simple as that.

The costs of taking another mother's child are enormous. You never feel 'right' about it. You always worry, if you take a child with a view to adoption, say, that the early experiences will affect the adult life. The social workers you deal with may or may not be people you can get along with. Most are informative, understanding and supportive. At times of crisis, though, they often seem to be sick, or on leave, or 'out of the office at the moment'.

The children themselves may resent you because they feel *you* are the ones who have wrenched them from their homes, and even badly treated children have a surprisingly strong bond with their 'real' Mum and Dad.

A hurt and confused foster child may often deliver the stinging blow: 'You don't really care about me. You only have me here for the money.' There is no real answer to that. A child's mind cannot grasp that payments made for food and clothing do not buy love. Social Workers are paid for their *time*; foster parents are not. Fostering is not a business, or an easy way to make money at home. You cannot go off duty and you cannot take a break for a few days. You live permanently on the job – and there is nowhere to escape to after a bad day.

So far the negatives. If the picture was really that bleak you would have to be a mug even to consider it. The negatives are simply easier to explain. But the positives, different perhaps for each person, are the ones you remember: the frightened child who trustingly takes your hand, the natural parent who confides their fear of being judged, and thanks you for being willing to help without judging; the sheer *fun* of riotous, colourful, tumbling children who will test you, anger you, and yet give you more than you could ever hope to achieve by yourself.

Life is more ordered for us now, more peaceful. The chaotic years described here are chapters of history. We did carry on short-term fostering for a while after Roger left us the second time, providing shelter for one or two bizarre characters who made Stella look positively staid by comparison! These days we follow the straight and easier path of long-term care, instead of the meandering helter-skelter of 'short-terming'.

There are very few books about fostering, either 'how-to' *or* 'how-we-did'. My own theory is that foster parents are far too busy doing it to write about it. To those many brave troopers who blaze this trail year after year, heroes with no recognition, we offer our unstinting admiration and support from the sidelines.

NFCA

The Foster Care Service Today

The National Foster Care Association is delighted to be associated with this book. It describes so graphically the experience of one foster family. Whilst every family, and every child will create their own different story, Beth Miller has managed to capture many elements which will ring true for other foster families. The valuable work which foster parents undertake has for too long gone unsung. When you read Beth's story you are seeing into the homes of some 30,000 families in the UK; we commend them to you for the invaluable service they offer to the children in care.

Foster care is a service available to thousands of children in care through the generosity of thousands of families who are willing to share themselves and their homes with these children and increasingly with the children's own families. Family life is the most natural environment for healthy growth and it is therefore considered to be the most appropriate form of care for the majority of children who cannot remain with their own families.

Children come into care for many reasons, mostly as a result of circumstances outside their control; family breakdown, housing, poverty, family ill-health and other such crises. Some come into care through the courts as a result of their own misbehaviour or being beyond the control of their own parents. They may stay in care only a matter of days, weeks or months. However, some remain for years, perhaps even most of their childhood. Each child will have his or her own personal needs, but all will require time and commitment; they will need to be made to feel secure and cared for and helped to deal with the sense of loss, separation and failure which many of them feel. Over 90,000 children in the UK are in care and of these over 40,000 find these needs met through foster care.

Foster families, just like the children, come from widely differing backgrounds, from every type of occupation – teachers, factory workers, unemployed, farmers, even MPs and Lords.

They may be married or single, including single men. They may be childless or already have children; they may be older with families who have grown up and left, or younger. There is a real need for a very wide cross-section of people to be available so that at any one time a real choice is possible, enabling children to be matched to the most appropriate family. Some families will be happier with certain kinds of children of a particular age or sex. Foster families are at liberty to make such decisions in line with their own feelings, skills, areas of interest and family circumstances. However, needs will vary from area to area. Homes for pre-school children are far less in demand than for adolescents. In some areas the predominant need is for families to care for children with different ethnic backgrounds. In this respect many more families with different ethnic backgrounds are being sought.

To become a foster parent can involve quite a tedious but very necessary process. People interested should seek further information either through meeting experienced foster parents, or applying for further information from their local social services or social work department, or a branch of one of the major voluntary child care organisations. A stamped addressed envelope to NFCA (address below) will supply some basic literature. Processes for approving foster parents will vary but must include visits by the social worker to meet the family individually and together, to view the home and to discuss various aspects of caring for someone else's child. Many agencies now make a preparation/training course available thus enabling new applicants to examine in more depth what foster care work entails.

Foster parenting today is about more than parenting. It is 'Parenting Plus', involving a partnership with social workers and their agencies, and very often, also with the parents. Placements of older children often require a different approach – more befriending and supporting. They may well have good memories of, and on-going contact with, their own families. The tasks involved can vary, as described by Beth. Some may be very short-term, others may last for years and, in a few cases, result in adoption.

There are allowances available to foster parents which vary according to age. They will also vary from agency to agency, there being no national scale except that which the NFCA promotes and advises as being appropriate. In addition, where a child has special needs involving costs over and above the basic allowances for 'normal' placements, enhanced payments can be made.

In a few agencies there are some special schemes which offer the foster parents a small fee for the work; these are normally related to particular hard-to-place children where special work is required.

As a result of more intensive efforts by social work departments far fewer pre-school children are being received into care. Homes are increasingly being sought for handicapped children, adolescents (including those who may have been in trouble with the law), emotionally disturbed children, those with behaviour disorders and groups of brothers and sisters. There is also a growth of what are known as 'respite care' schemes. In these cases the children are handicapped but living at home with their family. The placement with another family is to give the child's family 'respite', i.e. a break from the onorous task of the daily care of their child. These 'stays' are usually for an average of a couple of weeks at a time. For those who feel they can cope with handicapped children but cannot take on a long-term commitment this is a valuable way of helping.

The placement of children in foster homes is governed by government regulations. There are requirements to review regularly every placement, and to support the foster family. Increasingly, good practice is encouraging foster-parent involvement in decisions made about the care and progress of a child.

The National Foster Care Association offers membership to foster parents, social workers and others concerned about the quality of care for children in care. It is a UK-based organisation producing training material, publications, a quarterly magazine, information advice, counselling and a conciliation service, conferences and courses. It also concerns itself in a variety of ways with finding homes/families for children and liaises with the press and media.

If, after reading this book you think you might like to know more about foster care, please don't hesitate to enquire further. However, there are many who will read this book who cannot foster, for many different reasons. You can still help if you wish by making a donation to support the NFCA and its work. In the words of one child in care: 'It's not who borned you what matters, but who loves you.' Love, and care, can take many forms. You can help; we hope you will.

NATIONAL FOSTER CARE ASSOCIATION
Francis House, Francis Street, London SW1P 1DE.
Telephone: (01) 828 6266.